IMAGES
of America

GERSHWIN IN PITTSBURGH

George Gershwin (1898–1937). "Every musician who has studied modern music knows that jazz already has made a real contribution to our art," said Gershwin in 1926. (Billy Rose Theatre Division, the New York Public Library.)

On the Cover: Nixon Theatre, 1906. Pittsburgh's Nixon Theatre opened in 1903. It was the city's showplace for Broadway shows on tour, including most of George Gershwin's musicals. (Library of Congress Prints and Photographs Division.)

IMAGES
of America

GERSHWIN IN PITTSBURGH

Gregory Suriano

ARCADIA
PUBLISHING

ISBN 978-1-4671-0649-8

Published by Arcadia Publishing
Charleston, South Carolina

Printed in the United States of America

Library of Congress Control Number: 2020949265

For all general information, please contact Arcadia Publishing:
Telephone 843-853-2070
Fax 843-853-0044
E-mail sales@arcadiapublishing.com
For customer service and orders:
Toll-Free 1-888-313-2665

Visit us on the Internet at www.arcadiapublishing.com

In dedicating this book, there is no one more important to me—personally and inspirationally—than my wife, Sandra, who has endured my cultural obsessions for too many decades and wisely encouraged our family (with sons Daniel and Michael) to adopt Pittsburgh as our wondrous hometown.

Contents

ACKNOWLEDGMENTS

The following organizations and persons are gratefully acknowledged for providing information and documents, and as sources for illustrations: Rauh Jewish History Program and Archives, Senator John Heinz History Center; the Detre Library and Archives, Heinz History Center; the microfilm department and music department of Carnegie Library of Pittsburgh; Pittsburgh Symphony Orchestra; Pittsburgh Ballet Theatre; Curtis Theatre Collection, Hillman Library, University of Pittsburgh—especially *History of the Nixon Theatre* by Dorothea Breitwieser Gardner (PhD thesis, University of Pittsburgh, 1959); Museum of Modern Art Film Stills Archive; Billy Rose Theatre Division, the New York Public Library; Library of Congress Prints and Photographs Division; and University Library System (ULS) Digital Collections, University of Pittsburgh.

And for their knowledge and collaboration in our mutual work on various Gershwin exhibitions, lectures, concerts, and projects: Richard E. Rauh, Mike Plaskett, Richard Glazier, William C. Daw, Lisa Auel, Kathryn P. Logan, Martha L. Berg, Deborah Cavrak, Susan M. Melnick, and especially Marvin Hamlisch.

Finally, much appreciation and respect are due to the many authors whose carefully researched books on George Gershwin have proven invaluable—among them Edward Jablonski, Robert Kimball, Joan Peyser, Robert Pollack, Deena Rosenberg, and Charles Schwartz.

Unless otherwise noted, all images appear courtesy of the author.

Introduction

George Gershwin will be forever associated with New York City. This most American of composers derived his inspiration from Manhattan's energy, skyscrapers, jazz, nightlife, and the evolving Broadway-musical art form. Nevertheless, in the 1920s and 1930s, Gershwin and his music traversed the nation, often ending up in Pittsburgh.

Research on Gershwin's Pittsburgh connections has revealed a startling number of professional associates, touring Broadway shows, and personal concert performances that relate to the Steel City. For example, two of Gershwin's most important collaborators, George S. Kaufman and Oscar Levant, hailed from Pittsburgh. Stage director Ned Wayburn, born in Pittsburgh, basically gave Gershwin his start in New York, first as a rehearsal pianist and then as the composer of his major hit "Swanee." And when Gershwin spent his final year in Hollywood, it was to work on movies produced by Pittsburgh's Pandro S. Berman.

Not only did many of the composer's great Broadway musicals—*Lady, Be Good!*, *Oh, Kay!*, *Rosalie*, *Of Thee I Sing*, and others—play at the city's Nixon and Alvin Theatres during their post–New York road tours, but his grand opera *Porgy and Bess* was staged at the Nixon in 1936 to triumphant local notices. Gershwin himself, as pianist, made several concert stops at Pittsburgh venues, performing his *Rhapsody in Blue*, *Concerto in F*, *An American in Paris*, and other works. The most significant of these visits was the special concert in 1933 with the Pittsburgh Symphony that ended the blue law restrictions and inaugurated Sunday music performances in Pennsylvania.

Within the pages of this lovingly prepared and meticulously researched book is a cornucopia of images reflecting Gershwin's entire career as it relates to his many Pittsburgh-born associates and the city's now lost venues such as the Nixon and Alvin Theatres and the Syria Mosque. The chapters, and the images within them, are arranged in roughly chronological order, with the captions telling a continuous story of the composer's musical output from *The Passing Show of 1916* to his last songs for 1938's *The Goldwyn Follies*. Along with the visual treasures in this book, readers and even Gershwin scholars will discover facts, dates, and connections that are unexpected revelations.

ALVIN THEATRE. This c. 1937 photograph shows the Alvin Theatre on Sixth Street in Pittsburgh. Gershwin shows played here prior to its 1933 renovation. (Pittsburgh City Photographer Collection, University of Pittsburgh.)

One

OVERTURE

As a young man, Gershwin augmented his income as a song plugger at Remick's music house by making piano rolls and serving as a rehearsal pianist for various shows. During 1917 and 1918, Gershwin also accompanied theater singers in performances of their new songs. In November 1917, he was the pianist for Vivienne Segal at the Century Theatre Sunday Concerts series; she used two of his songs. He toured a few cities as accompanist to vaudeville performer Louise Dresser in February and March 1918 and then was the pianist for two "serious" recitals—featuring his most innovative songs and several piano preludes—by singers Eva Gauthier and Marguerite D'Alvarez.

New York musicals and plays of the time normally opened out of town as "tryouts," thus allowing some fine-tuning before their arrival on the Great White Way. After a successful Broadway run, a revue/musical might embark on a road tour to cities across America. Gershwin's earliest songs were heard in Pittsburgh during such tours, mainly at the Nixon and Alvin Theatres.

Occasionally, a Gershwin musical would not make it past the tryout city; *A Dangerous Maid*, with Vivienne Segal, played and closed in Pittsburgh in 1921. A few years earlier, notorious theater personality Nora Bayes had heard some of Gershwin's songs and wanted to use them in the tryout tour for her new show, *Look Who's Here*, soon to be *Ladies First*. Gershwin traveled with Bayes as her pianist during a six-week period in 1918, visiting Pittsburgh and other cities.

The director and dancing instructor Ned Wayburn was born in Pittsburgh, and through his stagings for a number of 1917–1920 shows, Gershwin was able to begin his career as a rehearsal/accompanying pianist and introduce some of his earliest songs. When *Hitchy-Koo of 1918*, staged by Wayburn, reached Pittsburgh, it also brought the vivacious Irene Bordoni, significant for her recordings and sheet music for two other shows with Gershwin songs that came to Pittsburgh in the early 1920s: *The French Doll* and *Little Miss Bluebeard*.

As for Wayburn, his 1919 *Demi Tasse Revue* introduced Gershwin's "Swanee," which, in the hands of Al Jolson the following year, sold millions of copies of sheet music and records—and made Gershwin a star.

George Gershwin Composing a Melody

George Gershwin, the Beginning. This image and caption were published in Thomas Edison's *Along Broadway* magazine in October 1920 to accompany an article interviewing the promising new composer. Gershwin is quoted as stating, "Operetta that represents the life and spirit of this country are decidedly my aim. After that may come opera, but I want all my work to have the one element of appealing to the great majority of our people."

Vivienne Segal (1897–1992), 1915. Vivienne Segal played an important role in Gershwin's early career, mainly as a star of the one Gershwin musical to play and close in Pittsburgh. Two of his first publicly performed compositions came with Segal—with the composer at the piano—choosing to sing his "You-oo Just You" (published by Remick, with Segal on the cover) and "There's More to the Kiss Than the X-X-X," for a special Sunday concert during the run of *Miss 1917*. Segal remained an important Broadway figure through the 1950s, notably starring with Pittsburgh's Gene Kelly in the 1940 musical *Pal Joey*; she also appeared in several movies and 1960s television series.

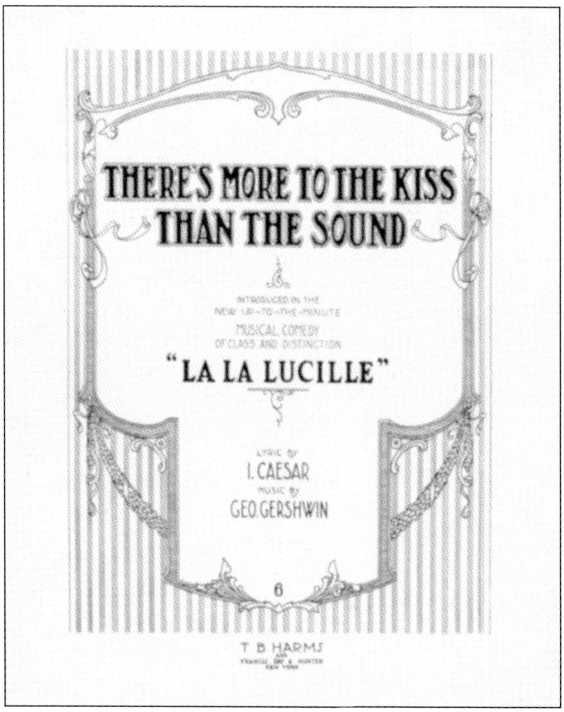

Sheet Music for "There's More to the Kiss Than the Sound." This early Gershwin song made the rounds (under two names: "There's More to the Kiss Than the Sound" and "There's More to the Kiss Than the X-X-X") in three separate productions, including *Good Morning, Judge*. While the published version shown here was for *La La Lucille* (1919), it was first heard under the "X" title for the Segal-Gershwin Century Theatre Sunday Concert that emerged from *Miss 1917*, for which Gershwin was the rehearsal pianist.

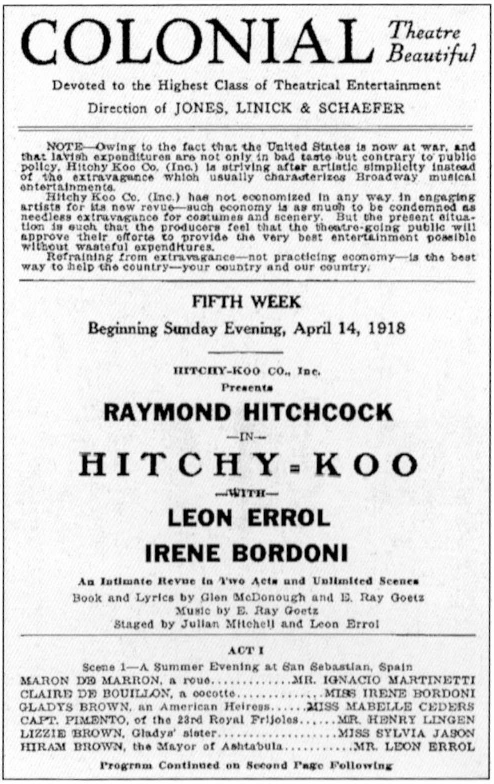

COLONIAL *Theatre Beautiful*

Devoted to the Highest Class of Theatrical Entertainment

Direction of JONES, LINICK & SCHAEFER

NOTE—Owing to the fact that the United States is now at war, and that lavish expenditures are not only in bad taste but contrary to public policy, Hitchy Koo Co. (Inc.) is striving after artistic simplicity instead of the extravagance which usually characterizes Broadway musical entertainments.

Hitchy Koo Co. (Inc.) has not economized in any way in engaging artists for its new revue—such economy is as much to be condemned as needless extravagance for costumes and scenery. But the present situation is such that the producers feel that the theatre-going public will approve their efforts to provide the very best entertainment possible without wasteful expenditures.

Refraining from extravagance—not practicing economy—is the best way to help the country—your country and our country.

FIFTH WEEK

Beginning Sunday Evening, April 14, 1918

HITCHY-KOO CO., Inc.

Presents

RAYMOND HITCHCOCK

—IN—

HITCHY-KOO

—WITH—

LEON ERROL

IRENE BORDONI

An Intimate Revue in Two Acts and Unlimited Scenes

Book and Lyrics by Glen McDonough and E. Ray Goetz

Music by E. Ray Goetz

Staged by Julian Mitchell and Leon Errol

ACT I

Scene 1—A Summer Evening at San Sebastian, Spain

MARON DE MARRON, a roue..............MR. IGNACIO MARTINETTI
CLAIRE DE BOUILLON, a cocotte..............MISS IRENE BORDONI
GLADYS BROWN, an American Heiress......MISS MABELLE CEDERS
CAPT. PIMENTO, of the 23rd Royal Frijoles......MR. HENRY LINGEN
LIZZIE BROWN, Gladys' sister....................MISS SYLVIA JASON
HIRAM BROWN, the Mayor of Ashtabula...........MR. LEON ERROL

Program Continued on Second Page Following

RAYMOND HITCHCOCK'S *HITCHY-KOO OF 1918* PROGRAM. Arriving in Pittsburgh in September 1918 during its post-Broadway tour, this show with two Gershwin songs—"You-oo Just You" (again) and "When the Armies Disband"—marked the composer's earliest contributions for a revue with both Ned Wayburn and Irene Bordoni. The program page shown is for a similar road-tour production at the Colonial Theatre in Chicago.

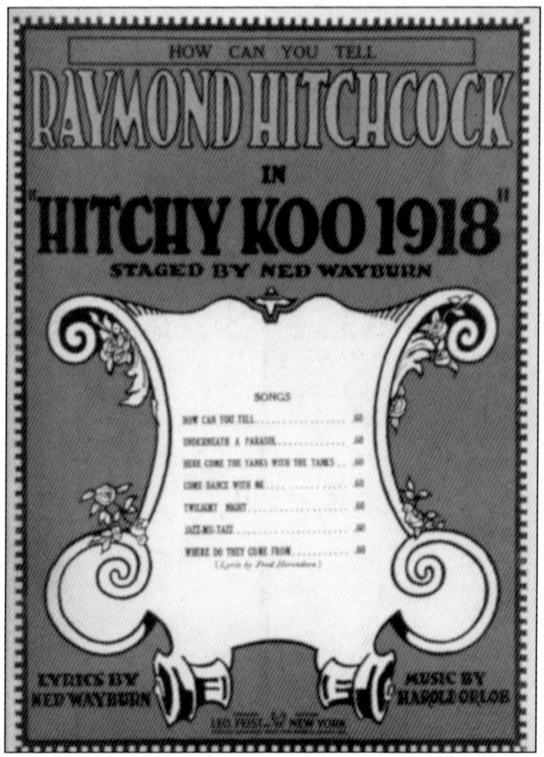

SHEET MUSIC FOR *HITCHY-KOO OF 1918*. This gorgeously designed sheet-music cover is for "How Can You Tell"—not a Gershwin song, but one with a lyric by Ned Wayburn, whose name is also prominently displayed for his staging of the show. Wayburn would play a seminal role in launching Gershwin's career.

Irene Bordoni (1885–1953). Like many early-1900s theatrical divas, Irene Bordoni was noted for her *au courant* fashions and overwhelming hats. Several of her stage vehicles with Gershwin songs (*Hitchy-Koo of 1918*, *The French Doll*, and *Little Miss Bluebeard*) came to Pittsburgh in the 1920s. The glamorous Corsican-born Art Deco goddess was a theater and recording star, an oft-photographed and caricatured personality, and a product-advertisement spokesperson. (Billy Rose Theatre Division, the New York Public Library.)

NED WAYBURN (1874–1942). Like Vivienne Segal, Ned Wayburn played an important role in Gershwin's early theatrical efforts. Wayburn was born in Pittsburgh ("where his parents were socially prominent," according to his 1925 book *The Art of Stage Dancing*) but gravitated for his career to Chicago and then to New York. A prodigious Broadway director since 1899, he staged the *Ziegfeld Follies* and *Ziegfeld Midnight Frolic* from 1916 through the early 1920s, as well as *Miss 1917*. Wayburn employed Gershwin as pianist for several of these shows, and also brought Bordoni and Gershwin together for *Hitchy-Koo of 1918*.

CAPITOL THEATRE PROGRAM, 1919. Wayburn produced and choreographed the 1919 show that introduced Gershwin's famous "Swanee." For the *Demi Tasse Revue*, Wayburn, the author of several editions of *The Art of Stage Dancing*, wrote the lyric for one of Gershwin's songs, "Come to the Moon" (as he did for *Hitchy-Koo of 1918* and other productions). Not only can Wayburn, a gentleman from the Steel City, be considered to have given George Gershwin his theatrical start, but the Ned Wayburn Studios of Stage Dancing trained such Broadway associates of the composer as Fred Astaire, Vivienne Segal, Ann Pennington, and Marilyn Miller.

Sheet Music for "Swanee," 1919. This was published in conjunction with Wayburn's Capitol Theatre *Demi Tasse Revue*, as was "Come to the Moon," with a similar cover. It is probable that Wayburn "discovered" Gershwin's song "Swanee" during the composer's stints as rehearsal pianist for the Wayburn-staged *Ziegfeld Midnight Frolic* series (1918 and 1919).

SHEET MUSIC FOR *SINBAD* ("SWANEE"), 1920. "Swanee," with a lyric by Gershwin's early collaborator Irving Caesar, became the composer's best-selling song hit when Al Jolson re-introduced (and recorded) it during the extensive national tour of his *Sinbad* show in 1920. Jolson brought *Sinbad* to Pittsburgh's Alvin Theatre in April 1920.

E. RAY GOETZ
Presents

"Vogues and Vanities"

A Musical Review of Revues, by Glen MacDonough and E. Ray Goetz,
Staged by
NED WAYBURN
Additional Musical Numbers by George Gershwin, George W. Meyer, Wm. M. Daly and Vincent Youmans.
Scenes and Costumes Designed by Homer Conant.

THE CAST:

Johnny Dooley, Anna Wheaton, Wm. Kent, Edith Hallor, Clifton Webb, Robert Emmett Keane, Helen Broderick, Evelyn Law, Lester Crawford, Maurice Diamond.

Ladies of the Ensemble

Margery Morrison, Jacqueline Hunter, Grace Jones, Lillian Mitchell, Helen Crawford, Violet Vale, Mabel Hastings, Bernice Dewey, Betty Walsh, Nan Rainsford, Josephine Rolfe, Carol Young, Helen Herendeen, Patricia Hope, Louise Saunders.

THE PROLOGUE.

Scene 1. "A Theatrical Manager's Office."

Mr. Showman (a manager)....................Mr. Keane
Mr. Penwiggle (an author)....................Mr. Webb

ACT I.

Scene 2. Outside the Hat Bazaar.

NO. 1—"Beautiful Feathers"....................Miss Hallor and Chorus.
Danse Divertisement....................Miss Law

Scene 3. The Hat Bazaar.

The Errand Boy....................Mr. Dooley
Charlie Meglip....................Mr. Kent
Mrs. Bingham, a widow....................Miss Broderick
Polly Parkes....................Miss Wheaton
No. 2—"If It Wasn't for Girls"....................Mr. Dooley and Chorus
No. 3—"On the Brim of Her Old Fashioned Bonnet"....................Miss Wheaton and Chorus

VOGUES AND VANITIES ROAD TOUR PROGRAM, 1920. Ned Wayburn staged *Vogues and Vanities*, a revue containing four Gershwin songs: "On the Brim of Her Old-Fashioned Bonnet," "The Baby Blues," "There Is Something Peculiar," and "The Futuristic Melody." The show never made it to Broadway but did have a long tryout tour. It played in Pittsburgh at the Alvin in October 1920 under the title *Piccadilly to Broadway*.

CLIFTON WEBB (1889–1966). *Piccadilly to Broadway* visited a number of cities during its unsuccessful tryout period, starting with Atlantic City in September 1920. Future movie star Clifton Webb—*Laura*, *The Razor's Edge*, *Cheaper by the Dozen*, *The Man Who Never Was*, *Three Coins in the Fountain*—was in the cast; he had been in a 1915 Ned Wayburn show, and in 1928 appeared in Gershwin's *Treasure Girl*.

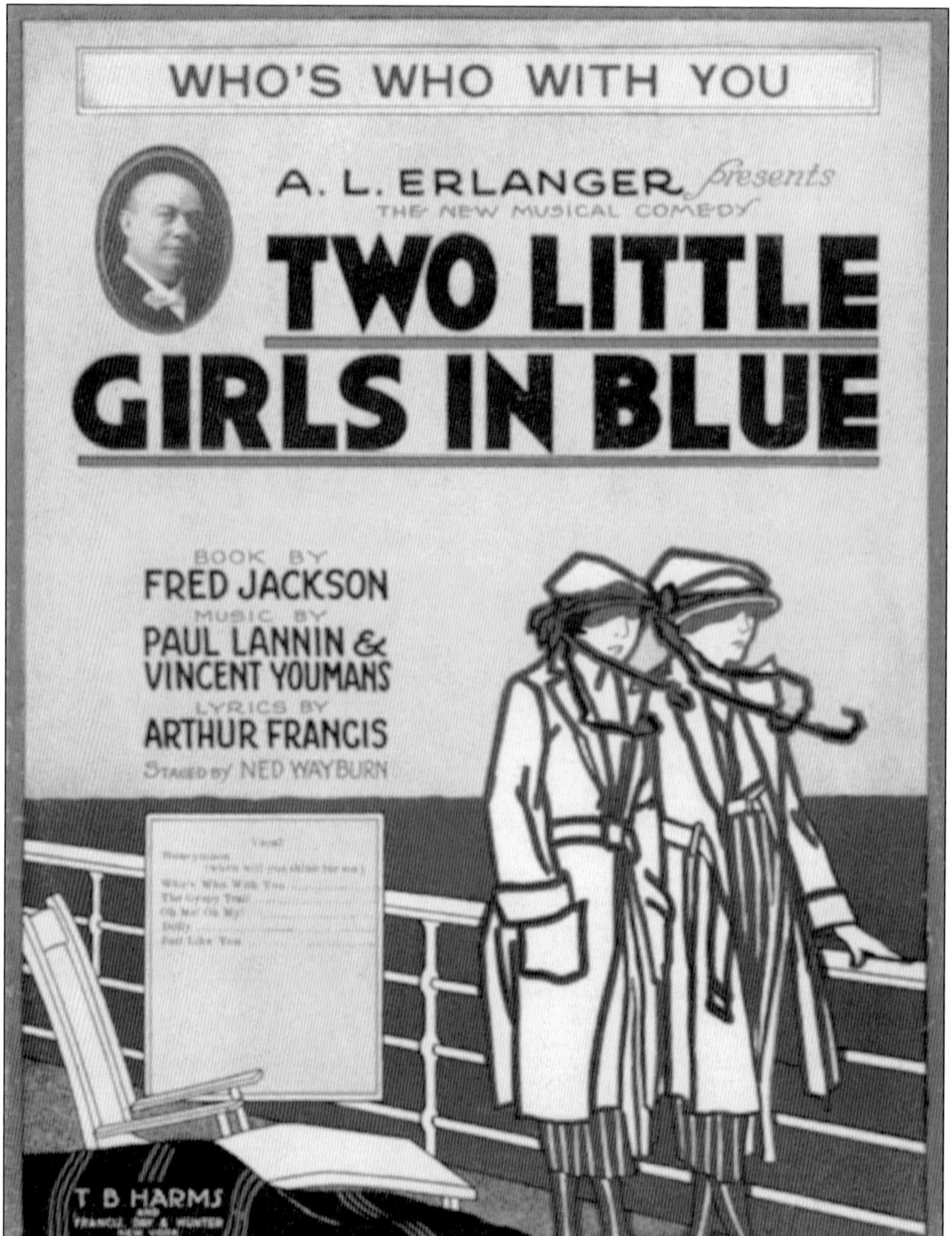

SHEET MUSIC FOR *TWO LITTLE GIRLS IN BLUE*, 1921. Another Ned Wayburn production, this musical played in Pittsburgh in December 1921. While George Gershwin did not write its music (Vincent Youmans and Paul Lannin provided that), it did have lyrics by Arthur Francis—an early pseudonym for George's soon-to-be-notable brother, Ira.

PITTSBURGH'S NIXON THEATRE, 1906. The Nixon, which opened in 1903, stood on Sixth Avenue and has sometimes been characterized as a French Beaux-Arts building. Samuel F. Nixon-Nirdlinger owned and operated the Nixon with partner Fred Zimmerman. For years, Sam Nixon's Theatrical Syndicate controlled bookings for important theaters all over the nation. The Nixon was the prime showplace for traveling Broadway shows, and in the 1910s, Florenz Ziegfeld favored it for tryouts of his grand *Follies* revues. It was the spectacular theatrical venue for most of George and Ira Gershwin's road-tour shows, including *Two Little Girls in Blue* and Irene Bordoni's starring vehicles. (Library of Congress Prints and Photographs Division.)

SHEET MUSIC FOR *THE FRENCH DOLL*, 1922. For this show at the Nixon in Pittsburgh in October 1922, Gershwin contributed one song, the languorously lovely "Do It Again." This strikingly designed cover depicts star Irene Bordoni in one of her huge hats.

LITTLE MISS BLUEBEARD ROAD TOUR PROGRAM, 1923. Bordoni's *Little Miss Bluebeard* with one Gershwin song played in Pittsburgh in March 1924. The program page here is from a similar touring production at another Nixon Theatre (same owner) in Atlantic City. The Atlantic City Nixon hosted the pre-Broadway tryouts for many Gershwin shows, including *La La Lucille*, *A Dangerous Maid*, *Tell Me More*, and the *Scandals* of 1921, 1923, and 1924. Most other Gershwin tryouts were in Boston or Philadelphia theaters.

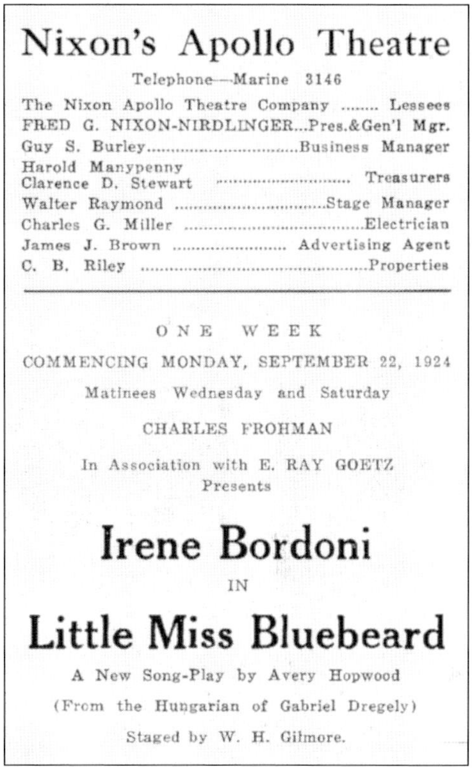

Nixon's Apollo Theatre

Telephone—Marine 3146

The Nixon Apollo Theatre Company .... Lessees
FRED G. NIXON-NIRDLINGER...Pres.&Gen'l Mgr.
Guy S. Burley.................................Business Manager
Harold Manypenny
Clarence D. Stewart .... Treasurers
Walter Raymond ....Stage Manager
Charles G. Miller ....Electrician
James J. Brown .... Advertising Agent
C. B. Riley ....Properties

ONE WEEK

COMMENCING MONDAY, SEPTEMBER 22, 1924

Matinees Wednesday and Saturday

CHARLES FROHMAN

In Association with E. RAY GOETZ
Presents

Irene Bordoni

IN

Little Miss Bluebeard

A New Song-Play by Avery Hopwood

(From the Hungarian of Gabriel Dregely)

Staged by W. H. Gilmore.

SHEET MUSIC FOR *LITTLE MISS BLUEBEARD*, 1923. Bordoni's *Little Miss Bluebeard* featured Gershwin's "I Won't Say I Will but I Won't Say I Won't"—a slightly naughty, half-spoken song recorded by Bordoni. Ira Gershwin, as Arthur Francis, teamed with Buddy DeSylva to write the lyric. The sheet music's cover art is one of the many caricatures done of the vivacious musical star.

AVERY HOPWOOD (1882–1928). Though not from Pittsburgh, Avery Hopwood is mentioned here as an interesting connection between Bordoni's *Little Miss Bluebeard* and another famous Pittsburgher, Mary Roberts Rinehart. A popular playwright of the 1920s, Hopwood was also the writer of Bordoni's *Naughty Cinderella* and of adaptations for numerous films, including *The Bat*, *Miss Bluebeard* (from the Bordoni show), *Gold Diggers of Broadway*, and *The Bat Whispers*.

MARY ROBERTS RINEHART (1876–1958). One of Pittsburgh's most famous and wealthiest women was mystery writer Mary Roberts Rinehart. Avery Hopwood collaborated with Rinehart on her hit murder-mystery play *The Bat*, which opened on Broadway in 1920 and haunted innumerable stages around the country for decades. The play spawned two early movies (1926 and 1930) and other later versions, and is renowned today as one of the inspirations for Bob Kane's creation of Batman. (Mary Roberts Rinehart Papers, University of Pittsburgh.)

Two

A Gershwin Song or Two at the Nixon and Alvin

The years of 1919 to 1923 recorded a flurry of musicals and revues with one or two songs contributed by Gershwin added to others' scores; these were called interpolations. Many of such obscure shows were nevertheless successes and made pre- or post-Broadway visits to the Alvin and Nixon Theatres in Pittsburgh.

Gershwin-related shows from this period that traveled from Manhattan to the Steel City were *The Passing Show of 1916* (Pittsburgh's initial exposure to Gershwin songs), *The Lady in Red*, *The Sweetheart Shop*, *The Dancing Girl*, *Blue Eyes*, *Piccadilly to Broadway*, *The Perfect Fool*, *Ed Wynn's Carnival*, and *Good Morning, Judge*.

Through these imports, many of George Gershwin's earliest songs were heard in Pittsburgh—and sometimes twice, recycled for different shows. For example, "Something About Love" and "Some Wonderful Sort of Someone" both turned up in two Pittsburgh tour shows: *Look Who's Here* (at the Alvin in 1918) and *The Lady in Red* (at the Alvin in 1919). "I Was So Young" in *Good Morning, Judge* (at the Alvin in 1919) returned in *Blue Eyes* (at the Alvin in 1921). "Spanish Love" was heard first in *Broadway Brevities of 1920* (at the Alvin in 1921) and then in *The Greenwich Village Follies of 1923* (at the Alvin in 1925).

Over at the Nixon, there were a few shows starring comedian Ed Wynn, a favorite of Gershwin. The long-running *Ed Wynn's Carnival* (another Ned Wayburn product) played in New York starting April 5, 1920, but had already reached Pittsburgh in its pre-Broadway phase in December 1919. There followed Wynn's *The Perfect Fool* (in New York through 1922), which ended up in Pittsburgh in September 1923.

Also heard at the Nixon was "Waiting for the Sun to Come Out" in *The Sweetheart Shop* (January 1920), marking the first time Ira Gershwin used his pseudonym—Arthur Francis—and the first published song by the Gershwin brothers words-and-music team.

A YOUTHFUL GEORGE GERSHWIN. This promotional photograph of Gershwin is from the early 1920s, when he had a lot of hair—and yes, one can judge the period of a Gershwin portrait by the change in his hairline.

SHEET MUSIC AND ADVERTISING CARD FOR *THE LADY IN RED*, 1919. This minor show had two songs by Gershwin and other interpolations by Jerome Kern and Walter Donaldson added to the general score by Robert Winterberg. Rescued from Gershwin's contributions to Nora Bayes's *Look Who's Here* were "Some Wonderful Sort of Someone" and "Something About Love." The latter song—oddly, without Gershwin credited—is the selection for the sheet music shown. *The Lady in Red* played in Pittsburgh at the Alvin Theatre in October 1919.

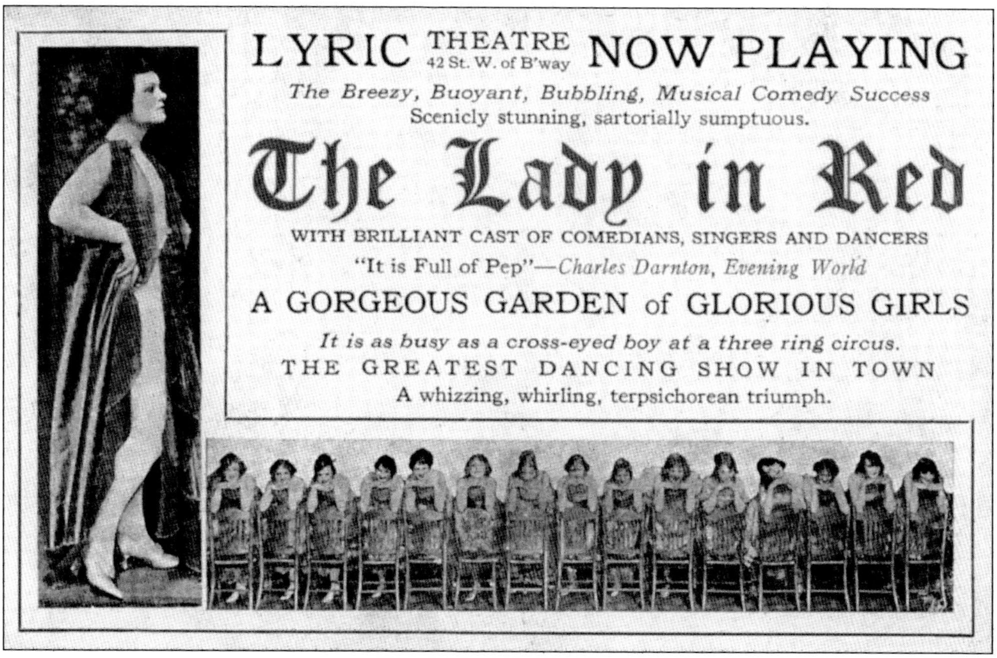

PROMOTIONAL HANDBILL FOR *GOOD MORNING, JUDGE*, 1919. Several splashy pages with scenes from this show make up this piece prepared for the road tour of the successful New York production. The tour reached the Alvin Theatre in Pittsburgh in November 1919. Gershwin again supplied two songs.

SHEET MUSIC FOR *GOOD MORNING, JUDGE*. One of Gershwin's contributions to the show was the lovely and popular ballad "I Was So Young, You Were So Beautiful." The lyricist (of two) was Irving Caesar, a frequent Gershwin song-partner who wrote the words for "Swanee." The second song was a returning "There's More to the Kiss Than the X-X-X." "I Was So Young" was reprised in another (very obscure) show, *Blue Eyes* of 1921, which played that same year at the Alvin, with a second Gershwin tune, "Wanting You."

SHEET MUSIC FOR *SNAPSHOTS OF 1921*. This revue played in New York and starred Lew Fields and the singer Gershwin accompanied in a 1918 tour for *Look Who's Here* (Pittsburgh included), Nora Bayes. Bayes is shown on the cover in her typical flamboyant headgear. In standard Bayes fashion, she quit the show before the tour, which reached the Steel City in November 1921. Gershwin songs recycled from 1920's *Piccadilly to Broadway* (also known as *Vogues and Vanities*, tryout at the Alvin) were "The Baby Blues," "On the Brim of Her Old-Fashioned Bonnet," and "The Futuristic Melody."

SHEET MUSIC FOR *THE SWEETHEART SHOP*, 1920. Gershwin's single song contribution to *The Sweetheart Shop* was "Waiting for the Sun to Come Out." This was a significant piece, for it was the first published song by the Gershwin brothers team. The show had a very successful pre-Broadway tour, bringing it to the Nixon Theatre in January 1920 (before its less successful two-month run in New York starting in August 1920).

STARS OF *THE SWEETHEART SHOP*. Two photographs (upper left and upper right) captioned "Charming Group from *The Sweetheart Shop*" and "Dainty Helen Ford in *The Sweetheart Shop*" were part of a magazine picture spread featuring current New York theatrical players. This appeared in the November 1920 issue of Edison's *Along Broadway*.

UNA FLEMING (1906–1964) IN *THE SWEETHEART SHOP*. Actor and dancer Una Fleming is known only for a few Broadway productions just after World War I, including *The Sweetheart Shop*, *Her Family Tree*, and *The Velvet Lady*. She made one movie, *The Talk of the Town*, released in 1918. (Jerome Robbins Dance Division, the New York Public Library and George Moffett.)

Sheet Music for *Broadway Brevities of 1920*. The *Pittsburgh Press* publicized *Broadway Brevities* as coming to the Alvin Theatre in mid-April 1921. The two Gershwin songs featured were "Spanish Love" and "Lu Lu." "Spanish Love" reappeared in *The Greenwich Village Follies of 1923* and again at the Alvin in January 1925.

Pittsburgh's Alvin Theatre, 1906. The Alvin Theatre, on Sixth Street in downtown Pittsburgh (in today's Cultural District), opened in September 1891 and closed in 1933 for a major renovation; it reopened in August 1934. After a 1940 roof collapse, it reappeared in April 1942 as the J.P. Harris Theatre. This is a photograph of the original building facade, around 1906. Gershwin's Broadway shows that made it to the Alvin would have played in this building. (Library of Congress Prints and Photographs Division.)

Ed Wynn (1886–1966). Wynn—a Pennsylvanian, though not from Pittsburgh—was one of the most popular comedians and theater performers of the 1910s and 1920s, and beyond. Gershwin was apparently an admirer of Wynn, who figured in several shows with the composer's songs: *The Passing Show of 1916*, *The Perfect Fool*, and *Ed Wynn's Carnival*. In fact, Gershwin actually adopted the pseudonym "Bert Wynn" to record some piano rolls early in his career. Ed Wynn produced and wrote his own shows and was heard on the radio in the 1930s. He later acted in many Disney films.

Sheet Music for *Ed Wynn's Carnival*, 1920. The long-running *Ed Wynn's Carnival* played in New York starting April 5, 1920, but had already reached Pittsburgh in its pre-Broadway phase in December 1919 at the Nixon. Evidence suggests it probably returned to the Steel City in December 1920. Most likely, Ned Wayburn supported the inclusion of Gershwin's song "Oo, How I Love to Be Loved by You" (unused from *La La Lucille*) in *Carnival*. For Wynn's *The Perfect Fool* (in Pittsburgh at the Nixon in September 1923), there were two songs by Gershwin.

Three

A Lady, a Maid, and Gershwin

Vaudeville empress Nora Bayes heard some of Gershwin's songs in 1918 and wanted to use them in the tryout tour for her new show *Look Who's Here*, ultimately retitled *Ladies First*. Gershwin traveled with Bayes as her pianist in fall 1918; the cities included Trenton, Cleveland, Pittsburgh, and Baltimore. When *Ladies First* opened successfully in New York on October 24, 1918, Gershwin was glad to be rid of Bayes, who was demanding and often insulting.

Attending one of the performances of *Look Who's Here* was a young boy who would turn up in New York at Gershwin's apartment in the mid-1920s and soon become his musical alter ego. A young Oscar Levant saw Bayes and Gershwin on stage in Pittsburgh in 1918, later recalling about the pianist in his 1940 autobiography *A Smattering of Ignorance*, "I had never heard such fresh, brisk, unstudied, completely free and inventive playing." The *Pittsburgh Gazette Times* (September 3, 1918) gave the show a good review, stating, "Miss Bayes puts expression and emphasis into the several songs given her," and pointing out Gershwin's "Wonderful Someone."

The most significant of George Gershwin's rehearsal-pianist outings was for Pittsburgh-born Ned Wayburn's *Miss 1917*, where he met his idol, Jerome Kern (the show's composer), and its star, Vivienne Segal. In November 1917, he accompanied Segal at the related Century Theatre Sunday Concerts series; she sang two of his songs.

In 1921, Pittsburgh continued as the venue for Gershwin firsts. Vivienne Segal's new vehicle was to be a Gershwin musical, *A Dangerous Maid*. It embarked on a pre-Broadway road tour and, on April 11, 1921, opened at the Nixon Theatre in Pittsburgh. The *Pittsburgh Press* previewed it, with large photographs of the stars filling a third of a page above the fold. Small articles discussed performers in the show, singling out Segal.

A Dangerous Maid closed in Pittsburgh. One of the most obscure Gershwin shows, it never made it to Broadway. Two of its songs, however, did turn up in a successful musical. *Primrose*, a Gershwin production that was created for London, contained songs last heard in Pittsburgh: "Boy Wanted" and "The Sirens" (also known as "Four Little Sirens").

George Gershwin. This photograph was most likely taken aboard a ship to London for a trip to supervise one of Gershwin's specifically British shows. (Library of Congress Prints and Photographs Division.)

Nora Bayes (1880–1928). Nora Bayes was a popular theater star of the first few decades of the 20th century. Like Irene Bordoni, she was noted for her huge and extravagant headdresses—as well as her diva-like personality; "difficult" would be an appropriate way to describe her reputation. She liked some of Gershwin's songs, and the composer agreed to be her pianist on a pre-Broadway road tour of her show *Look Who's Here/Ladies First*. In his 1940 autobiography *A Smattering of Ignorance*, Gershwin's friend Oscar Levant recalled that at the time, Gershwin "remarked that Bayes was constantly complaining that his playing distracted her from what she was trying to do, and that she frequently threatened to get somebody else." (Library of Congress Prints and Photographs Division.)

CENTRAL THEATRE
B'way & 47th St. Phone Bryant 17.
Evgs. 8.30. Mats. Wed. & Sat. 2.30.
ARTHUR HAMMERSTEIN'S
Newest Musical Play
"SOMEBODY'S SWEETHEART"

44th ST. Theatre W. of Broadway
Phone Bryant 729
Evgs., 8.30 Mats., Wed. & Sat. 2.30
AL. JOLSON
In SINBAD

SHUBERT THEATRE, 44th, W. of B'way. Phone Bryant 8439.
Evgs. 8.15. Mats. Wed. and Sat. 2.15
'Good Morning, Judge'
WITH
GEORGE HASSELL | MOLLIE KING | CHARLES KING

CASINO B'way & 39th St.
Phone 3846 Greeley
Evgs. 8.15. Mats. Wed. & Sat. 2.15
A MERRY MUSICAL ROMANCE
SOME TIME
with ED. WYNN.

BIJOU Theatre, 45th, West of B'way
Phone Bryant 430 Evgs. 8.30
Mats. Wed. & Sat. 2.30
A New Farce Comedy
A SLEEPLESS NIGHT

Personally in
FOREVER AFTER

WinterGarden Broadway and 50th Street
Phone Circle 2330
Evgs. at 8. Mats. Tues., Thurs. & Sat. at 2
LEE & J. J. SHUBERT Present the
Winter Garden's Midwinter Extravaganza
MONTE CRISTO, JR.

NORA BAYES THEATRE
44th St., W. of Broadway.
Evgs. 8.15. Mats Wed. & Sat. 2.15
LAST WEEK
NORA BAYES
AT HER BEST IN LADIES FIRST

BOOTH THEATRE
45th, W. of Broadway. Evenings 8.30
Matinees Wed & Sat. 2.30
THE WOMAN IN ROOM 13

39th St. THEATRE
East of B'way. Phone Bryant 413.
Evgs. 8.30. Mats. Wed. & Sat. 2.30
GEORGE BROADHURST Presents
THE LAUGH PLAY
Keep It To Yourself

THEATER-ADVERTISEMENT PAGE WITH *LADIES FIRST*, 1919. This theater-directory page appeared in the *New York Dramatic Mirror* on March 15, 1919. *Ladies First* was advertised along with two other Gershwin-related vehicles: *Sinbad* with Al Jolson and *Good Morning, Judge*. The Bayes show had opened in New York in October 1918 and enjoyed a respectable 164 performances.

SHEET MUSIC FOR *LOOK WHO'S HERE*, 1918. This reflects Nora Bayes's first title for her show (as presented in Pittsburgh in September 1918), better known as *Ladies First*. The song is Gershwin's "Some Wonderful Sort of Someone," with a lyric by Schuyler Greene. The review in the Pittsburgh *Gazette Times* singled out Gershwin's "Wonderful Someone."

STREET SCENE WITH THE ALVIN THEATRE, 1915. The Alvin was second to the Nixon in attracting important New York shows, and the show that would become *Ladies First* played there in 1918. Gershwin, as pianist, traveled to several cities with Bayes during a six-week period (September–October) in 1918. The *Pittsburgh Press* heralded the arrival at the Alvin Theatre of *Look Who's Here* on September 1, 1918. It was *Ladies First* that opened successfully in New York on October 24, 1918, continuing there through March 1919. The Alvin is hidden (note the small domed marquee) on the near left side of this picture that shows a congested and trolley-tracked Sixth Street in about 1915. (Pittsburgh City Photographer Collection, University of Pittsburgh.)

SYNOPSIS

ACT I

Living Room of Aunt Jim's Apartment—Morning

ACT II

Gardens of Betty Burt and Benton Holmes—Afternoon

ACT III

Drawing-room in Betty's Home—Evening

MUSICAL NUMBERS

Oscar Radin .... Conductor

ACT I

1 Happy Days .... Burt, Tody, Betts, McGuirk
2 Crowd of Girls .... Burt and girls
3 Waiting for This .... Holmes
4 Wonderful Someone .... Betty
5 Build a Home .... Betty and Holmes
6 War Garden .... Burt and Doris
7 Finale.

ACT II

1 Ensemble .... Doris and Girls
2 Velvet .... Burt
3 What a Girl Can Do .... Betty and Girls
4 Home Life .... Betty and Holmes
5 Duet .... Aunt Jim and Uncle Tody
6 Take a Walk .... D. C. Washington
7 We'll Be There .... Aunt Jim and Girls
8 Finale.

ACT III

1 What's the Use? .... Benton Holmes
2 Songs by .... Benton Holmes and Washington
3 American Rag .... Larry Burt
4 Me and You .... Betty and Benton
5 Good Bye, America .... Betty

Interiors designed and executed by Suffolk & Ott, Inc.
Gowns by Bendel.
Scenes designed and painted by Dodge & Castle
The Knabe Piano is used by Miss Bayes

LADIES FIRST PROGRAM. A listing of the musical numbers in this Bayes show reveals a few interesting variations on Gershwin's two listed contributions, naming one song erroneously "Wonderful Someone" and the other "American Rag" (known formally as "The Real American Folk Song"). A third, "Something About Love," was also among the Gershwin songs heard during the fall 1918 *Look Who's Here* tryout tour; it eventually ended up in 1919's *The Lady in Red*.

A. BALDWIN SLOANE (1872–1925). Composer of record for *Ladies First*, Alfred Baldwin Sloane was a prominent Broadway songwriter during the first three decades of the 20th century. Gershwin had a lot to say about his experience with Sloane and *Ladies First*. According to Andrea Peyser in her 1993 book *The Memory of All That: The Life of George Gershwin*, Gershwin wrote from Baltimore to Irving Caesar (lyricist of "Swanee" and other Gershwin tunes), "Baldwin Sloane who wrote the music to the show gets 3 percent royalty, there are 9 interpolated songs and 8 songs by Sloane. He told me he got $400 for Pittsburgh week—including one day in Trenton. Pretty soft for him."

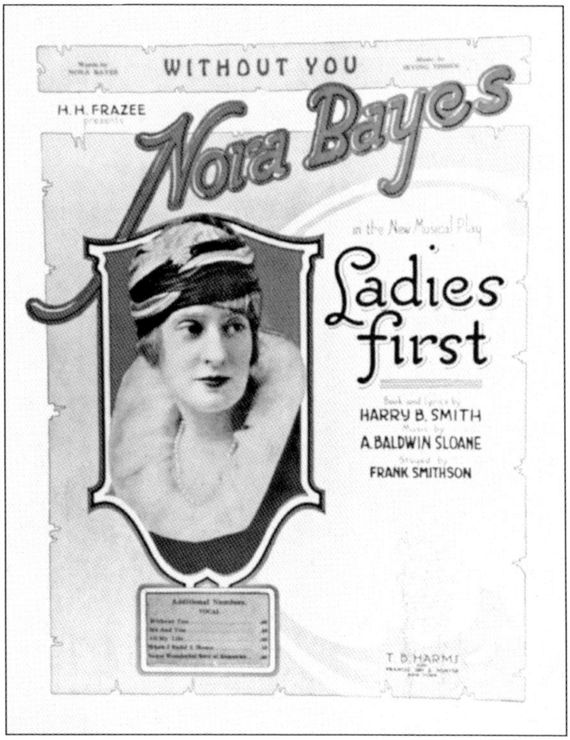

SHEET MUSIC FOR *LADIES FIRST*. This version of the music sheet reflects the final title of the Bayes show and features yet another contributor to the Baldwin Sloane "score," Irving Fisher, with words by Bayes herself. For some reason, the Broadway *Ladies First* eliminated a few of Gershwin's songs.

OSCAR LEVANT (1906–1972). Concert pianist, movie actor, and noted "wit," Oscar Levant was George Gershwin's friend and accompanist. Levant began his appreciation for the Gershwin sound as a young "gallery spectator" at *Look Who's Here* in Pittsburgh. In *A Smattering of Ignorance*, Levant recalled, "After one chorus of the first song my attention left Bayes and remained fixed on the playing of the pianist. I had never heard such fresh, brisk, unstudied, completely free and inventive playing—all within a consistent frame that set off her singing perfectly."

VIVIENNE SEGAL, C. 1917. Pennsylvanian Vivienne Segal (born in Philadelphia) began her Broadway career in 1915 with Sigmund Romberg's *The Blue Paradise*. She championed Gershwin's music from their earliest relationship, in *Miss 1917*. With *A Dangerous Maid* of 1921, she was able to perform in a complete Gershwin musical. (Library of Congress Prints and Photographs Division.)

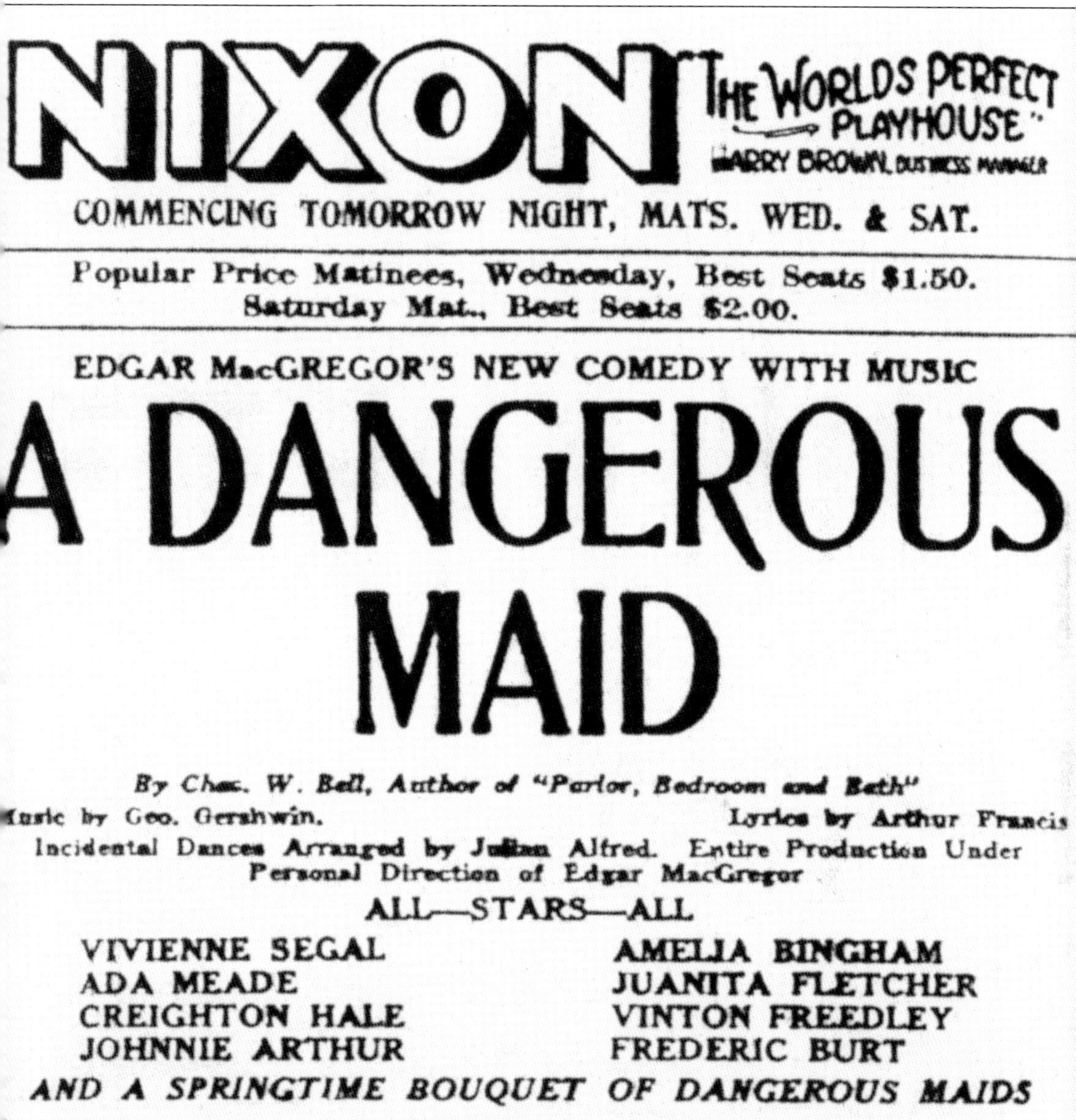

PITTSBURGH ADVERTISEMENT FOR *A DANGEROUS MAID.* Vivienne Segal was a featured player in this show, which came to Pittsburgh as part of its pre-Broadway tryout period. It ran at the Nixon Theatre starting on April 11, 1921, closing there on April 16—and going nowhere else. Never reaching Broadway, two of its songs were salvaged for a longer trip: to London for another Gershwin show, *Primrose.* This *Dangerous Maid* advertisement appeared in the *Pittsburgh Press* on April 10, 1921.

NEWSPAPER LAYOUT FOR *A DANGEROUS MAID* AT THE NIXON THEATRE. This pictorial layout of the personalities in *A Dangerous Maid* was published in the *Pittsburgh Press* on April 10, 1921. Vivienne Segal is pictured here along with Ada Meade and Creighton Hale. Two accompanying articles reviewed the show, calling it "a musical production that has Vivienne Segal among its principals—Vivienne in a role specially devised for her."

SHEET MUSIC FOR *A DANGEROUS MAID*, 1921. This song by Gershwin is "Just to Know You Are Mine." Others published (listed in the box on the cover) were "Dancing Shoes," "Some Rain Must Fall," and "Boy Wanted." Also in the show were "The Simple Life," "True Love," "The Sirens," and "Anything for You."

VINTON FREEDLEY (1891–1969). Producer and theater owner Vinton Freedley, together with his partner Alex Aarons, sponsored many of the Gershwins' musicals, mainly at their own Broadway theater, the Alvin. Freedley visited Pittsburgh as a cast member of *A Dangerous Maid* during its short run in the city. This rare photograph of Freedley in his early days (he had a long career in theater, movie, and television production) was reproduced in *Theatre Magazine* in June 1925.

IRA GERSHWIN (1896–1983). Brother Ira was George's show-writing partner for much of the 1920s and 1930s. Before *A Dangerous Maid*, Ira felt it necessary to write lyrics, with George and other composers, under the name Arthur Francis (derived from their two other siblings). Although Ira was still using this nom-de-plume, *A Dangerous Maid* was the first complete musical with songs by the Gershwin brothers.

Nixon Theatre Postcard, Detail. The Nixon was the prime showplace for traveling Broadway shows, and in the 1910s, Florenz Ziegfeld favored it for tryouts of his lavish *Follies* revues. In New Jersey, Sam Nixon also acquired an Atlantic City theater, which opened as Nixon's Apollo Theatre in April 1908. Among the many Gershwin musicals that had tryouts there was *A Dangerous Maid*, which closed in Pittsburgh.

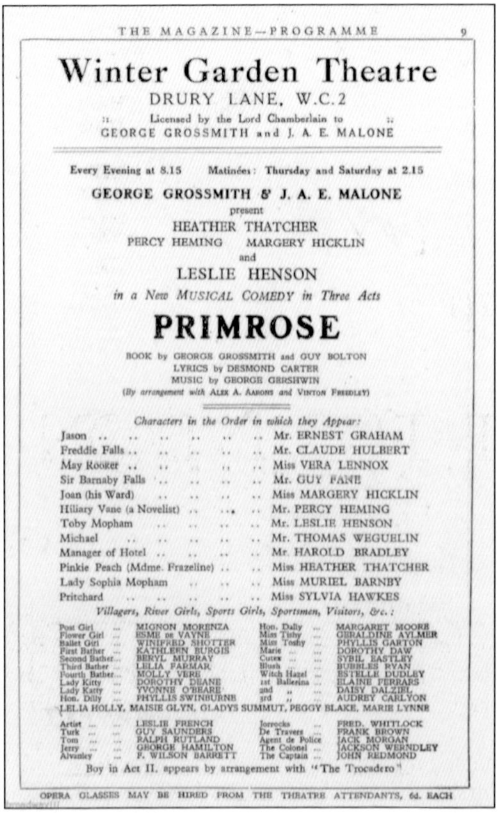

THE MAGAZINE—PROGRAMME 9

Winter Garden Theatre

DRURY LANE, W.C.2

Licensed by the Lord Chamberlain to
GEORGE GROSSMITH and J. A. E. MALONE

Every Evening at 8.15 Matinées: Thursday and Saturday at 2.15

GEORGE GROSSMITH & J. A. E. MALONE
present
HEATHER THATCHER
PERCY HEMING MARGERY HICKLIN
and
LESLIE HENSON
in a New MUSICAL COMEDY in Three Acts

PRIMROSE

BOOK by GEORGE GROSSMITH and GUY BOLTON
LYRICS by DESMOND CARTER
MUSIC by GEORGE GERSHWIN
(*By arrangement with* ALEX A. AARONS *and* VINTON FREEDLEY)

Characters in the Order in which they Appear:

Jason	Mr. ERNEST GRAHAM
Freddie Falls	Mr. CLAUDE HULBERT
May Rooker	Miss VERA LENNOX
Sir Barnaby Falls	Mr. GUY FANE
Joan (his Ward)	Miss MARGERY HICKLIN
Hiliary Vane (a Novelist)	Mr. PERCY HEMING
Toby Mopham	Mr. LESLIE HENSON
Michael	Mr. THOMAS WEGUELIN
Manager of Hotel	Mr. HAROLD BRADLEY
Pinkie Peach (Mdme. Frazeline)	Miss HEATHER THATCHER
Lady Sophia Mopham	Miss MURIEL BARNBY
Pritchard	Miss SYLVIA HAWKES

Villagers, River Girls, Sports Girls, Sportsmen, Visitors, &c.:

Post Girl	MIGNON MORENZA	Hon. Dally	MARGARET MOORE
Flower Girl	ESME DE VAYNE	Miss Tishy	GERALDINE AYLMER
Ballet Girl	WINIFRED SHOTTER	Miss Toshy	PHYLLIS GARTON
First Bather	KATHLEEN BURGIS	Marie	DOROTHY DAW
Second Bather	BERYL MURRAY	Cutex	SYBIL EASTLEY
Third Bather	LELIA FARMAR	Blush	BUBBLES RYAN
Fourth Bather	MOLLY VERE	Witch Hazel	ESTELLE DUDLEY
Lady Kitty	DOROTHY DEANE	1st Ballerina	ELAINE FERRARS
Lady Katty	YVONNE O'BEARE	2nd ,,	DAISY DALZIEL
Hon. Dilly	PHYLLIS SWINBURNE	3rd ,,	AUDREY CARLYON

LELIA HOLLY, MAISIE GLYN, GLADYS SUMMUT, PEGGY BLAKE, MARIE LYNNE

Artist	LESLIE FRENCH	Jorrocks	FRED. WHITLOCK
Turk	GUY SAUNDERS	De Travers	FRANK BROWN
Tom	RALPH RUTLAND	Agent de Police	JACK MORGAN
Jerry	GEORGE HAMILTON	The Colonel	JACKSON WERNDLEY
Alvanley	F. WILSON BARRETT	The Captain	JOHN REDMOND

Boy in Act II. appears by arrangement with "The Trocadero"

OPERA GLASSES MAY BE HIRED FROM THE THEATRE ATTENDANTS, 6d. EACH

PRIMROSE PROGRAM, 1924. *Primrose*, a mid-1920s London show (later traveling to Australia, but never to the United States) with music by Gershwin, used two of the songs from the musical *A Dangerous Maid*. The songs that did turn up in the very successful *Primrose* were "Boy Wanted" and "Four Little Sirens" (originally "The Sirens").

SCENE FROM *PRIMROSE*. Gershwin's music for this show was complex and inventive, with jazzy songs ("Boy Wanted" and "Naughty Baby") alternating with British-flavored pieces such as "Wait a Bit, Susie" and "The Mophams." An instrumental ballet sequence was among the musical's many recorded numbers released in England. This photograph was published in *Play Pictorial* in 1924.

Four

Scandals at the Nixon

After the string of revues and musicals with interpolated Gershwin songs that arrived at the Nixon and Alvin Theatres in the early 1920s (*The Passing Show of 1916*, *Hitchy-Koo of 1918*, *The Sweetheart Shop*, *The French Doll*, *Little Miss Bluebeard*, *Look Who's Here/Ladies First*, *Sinbad*, and *Good Morning, Judge*), the Nixon hosted most major all-Gershwin shows throughout the 1920s and 1930s, including 1921's *A Dangerous Maid*.

By the early 1920s, George Gershwin had become famous and wealthy, in no small part due to his worldwide hit song "Swanee" (heard in Pittsburgh via Al Jolson's *Sinbad* in April 1920). He continued to make his mark in a successful annual series of revues, *George White's Scandals*. He got his feet wet, so to speak, in preparation for the *Scandals*, with an all-Gershwin score for 1919's *Morris Gest's Midnight Whirl*, which contained seven of his numbers (it finally arrived in Pittsburgh in 1921).

All five of the Gershwin-scored *Scandals* toured, stopping at Pittsburgh's Nixon Theatre, and averaging 12 songs by the composer. The *Scandals* were slightly risqué revues along the lines of the *Ziegfeld Follies*. George White was a dancer and the impresario of this successful series, which continued to play annually well after Gershwin's participation ended and then became the basis of several movie musicals.

Among the *Scandals*' glamorous female dancers were Ann Pennington (its major headliner), Louise Brooks (later the captivating silent-movie star of *Pandora's Box*), and Dolores Costello (Pittsburgh born and soon to be a well-known movie star).

The *Scandals of 1920* (second annual) was Gershwin's first, in Pittsburgh in January 1921. While Gershwin's songs for these revues were not always his most inspired, a few were genuine groundbreakers for his mature and characteristic style.

The *Scandals of 1922* (fourth annual) opened in New York on August 28, 1922, and featured the Paul Whiteman Orchestra. This *Scandals* (in Pittsburgh starting January 15, 1923) introduced a classic early-Gershwin jazzy-blues showstopper, "I'll Build a Stairway to Paradise." The next day's *Pittsburgh Post* pointed out Whiteman's "weird near-human concoctions."

The sixth, and Gershwin's last, *Scandals* was the 1924 edition (in Pittsburgh January 1925), and from it came one of the composer's most enduring and beautiful ballads: "Somebody Loves Me."

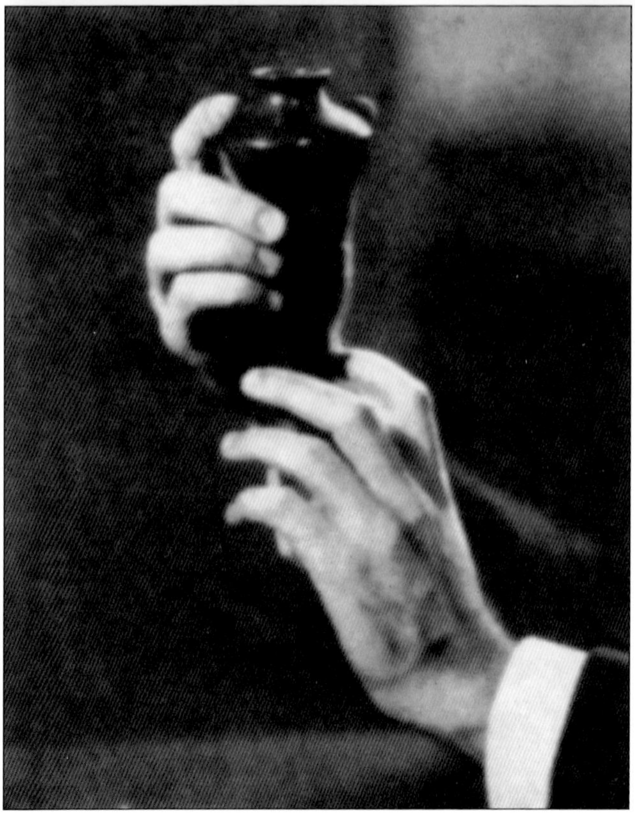

George Gershwin in a Contemplative Mood. These two photographs were part of a magazine layout for an article by Gershwin himself, "Jazz Is the Voice of the American Soul," published in *Theatre Magazine* in March 1927. The photograph at left is captioned "The Gershwin hands that have made the piano talk an entirely new language of music."

PROMOTIONAL HANDBILL FOR THE *CENTURY MIDNIGHT WHIRL*, 1919. This piece advertised the original New York production of the *Midnight Whirl* at the Century Grove on the roof of the Century Theatre. *The New York Times* reviewed the show with this headline on December 14, 1918: "Midnight Whirl Glitter: New Revue on Century Roof Is Lively and Funny." Unlike other shows of the period for which Gershwin contributed one or two interpolated songs, the *Midnight Whirl* seemed a rehearsal for the complete scores he would soon provide for the annual *George White's Scandals* revues.

SHEET MUSIC FOR THE *CENTURY MIDNIGHT WHIRL*. Bessie McCoy Davis was the headliner for the *Century Midnight Whirl.* Also known as *Morris Gest's Midnight Whirl*, it came to Pittsburgh's Nixon Theatre in March 1921. The Gershwin score consisted of "The League of Nations," "Doughnuts," "Poppyland," "I'll Show You a Wonderful World," "Limehouse Nights," "Let Cutie Cut Your Cuticle," and "Baby Dolls."

GEORGE WHITE (1891–1968). White was a dancer in one of Gershwin's first "rehearsal-pianist" efforts, *Miss 1917*. His extravagant *Scandals* revues, the first of which was in 1919, were certainly the best of several *Ziegfeld Follies* competitors. White was responsible for popularizing such dance crazes as the Turkey Trot and the Black Bottom. Among the entertainers who graced White's stage over the years were Ann Pennington, Dolores Costello, Ethel Merman, W.C. Fields, Helen Morgan, and Alice Faye. White produced annual *Scandals* through the 1930s, and Gershwin's five years as their composer certainly contributed to their increasing success.

SCENE FROM *GEORGE WHITE'S SCANDALS*. The *Scandals* in the early 1920s boasted Gershwin scores, and this stage-scene photograph gives a flavor of the line of glamorous dancers featured in these revues. Producer/dancer White is shown leading the group in the center. (Billy Rose Theatre Division, the New York Public Library.)

SCANDALS OF 1920 ROAD TOUR PROGRAM. This program page describes a *Scandals* touring production at the Colonial Theatre in Boston, similar to one that played in Pittsburgh at the Nixon Theatre in January 1921. "On My Mind the Whole Night Long" was noted at the time for its jazzy (or bluesy) qualities. That song, "Idol Dreams," and "Scandal Walk" were recorded by Gershwin as piano rolls in summer 1920, with "On My Mind" listed as a "Blues–Fox Trot."

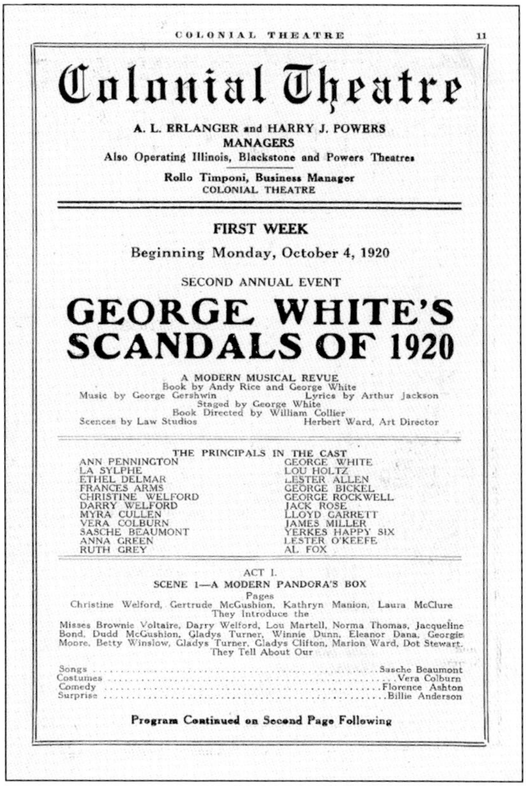

COLONIAL THEATRE 11

Colonial Theatre

A. L. ERLANGER and HARRY J. POWERS
MANAGERS
Also Operating Illinois, Blackstone and Powers Theatres

Rollo Timponi, Business Manager
COLONIAL THEATRE

FIRST WEEK

Beginning Monday, October 4, 1920

SECOND ANNUAL EVENT

GEORGE WHITE'S SCANDALS OF 1920

A MODERN MUSICAL REVUE
Book by Andy Rice and George White
Music by George Gershwin — Lyrics by Arthur Jackson
Staged by George White
Book Directed by William Collier
Scences by Law Studios — Herbert Ward, Art Director

THE PRINCIPALS IN THE CAST

ANN PENNINGTON	GEORGE WHITE
LA SYLPHE	LOU HOLTZ
ETHEL DELMAR	LESTER ALLEN
FRANCES ARMS	GEORGE BICKEL
CHRISTINE WELFORD	GEORGE ROCKWELL
DARRY WELFORD	JACK ROSE
MYRA CULLEN	LLOYD GARRETT
VERA COLBURN	JAMES MILLER
SASCHE BEAUMONT	YERKES HAPPY SIX
ANNA GREEN	LESTER O'KEEFE
RUTH GREY	AL FOX

ACT I.

SCENE 1—A MODERN PANDORA'S BOX

Pages
Christine Welford, Gertrude McGushion, Kathryn Manion, Laura McClure
They Introduce the
Misses Brownie Voltaire, Darry Welford, Lou Martell, Norma Thomas, Jacqueline Bond, Dudd McGushion, Gladys Turner, Winnie Dunn, Eleanor Dana, Georgie Moore, Betty Winslow, Gladys Turner, Gladys Clifton, Marion Ward, Dot Stewart.
They Tell About Our

Songs .... Sasche Beaumont
Costumes .... Vera Colburn
Comedy .... Florence Ashton
Surprise .... Billie Anderson

Program Continued on Second Page Following

SHEET MUSIC FOR THE SCANDALS OF 1920. This second annual edition of the *Scandals* was Gershwin's first for George White, featuring such songs as "Idle Dreams" (some sheet-music versions have the title as "Idol Dreams," which is in keeping with a theme of that sequence in the revue). The show's major hit was an early piece in Gershwin's jazzy style, "Scandal Walk." A very young Alfred Newman—later one of the greatest of Hollywood film composers—conducted the orchestra.

SHEET MUSIC FOR THE *SCANDALS* OF 1921. Gershwin's "South Sea Isles" was written for this third annual edition, headlining—even on the sheet-music cover—main *Scandals* star Ann Pennington. "Drifting Along with the Tide" was the hit song (inspiring a Gershwin piano roll) from that year's revue, which visited Pittsburgh's Nixon Theatre in January 1922.

ANN PENNINGTON (1893–1971). After five annual editions with the *Ziegfeld Follies*, dancer Ann Pennington became the star attraction of *George White's Scandals* starting with the first in 1919. Gershwin had been the rehearsal pianist for Ned Wayburn's *Miss 1917* and the *Ziegfeld Follies of 1918*, both with Pennington. She soon became one of the most recognizable of all Broadway performers and was identified with both the Charleston and Black Bottom dance crazes. This publicity photograph by Edward Thayer Monroe is from 1921, as she was starring in the third *Scandals*.

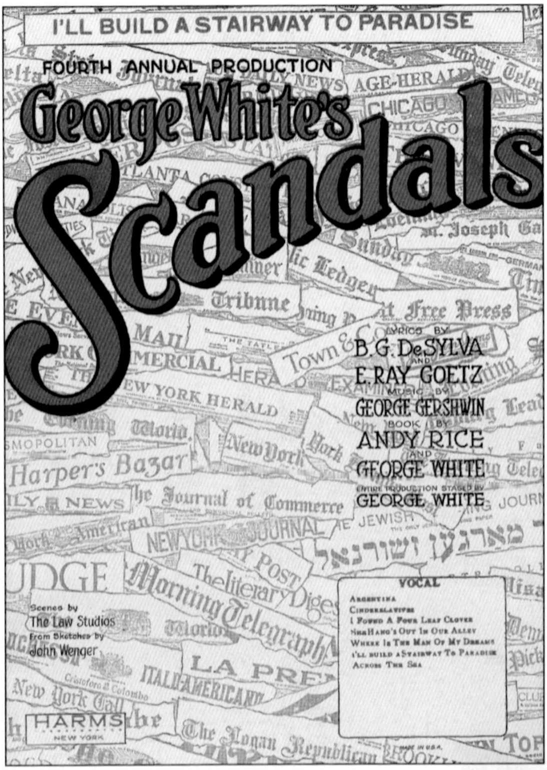

SHEET MUSIC FOR THE *SCANDALS* OF *1922*. With the fourth annual edition of the *Scandals*, the mature Gershwin was breaking through—with prefigurations of *Rhapsody in Blue* and *Lady, Be Good!* There were the unsuccessful and short-lived *Blue Monday* mini-opera and the jazzy, rhythmic explosion of "I'll Build a Stairway to Paradise." The revue was also notable for featuring W.C. Fields. The *Scandals* played in Pittsburgh at the Nixon Theatre starting January 15, 1923.

PAUL WHITEMAN (1890–1967) IN THE *SCANDALS* OF *1922*. The *Scandals of 1922* opened in New York on August 28, 1922, and featured Paul Whiteman and His Orchestra. Whiteman's exposure to Gershwin's music in this *Scandals* prompted the bandleader's decision to commission what became *Rhapsody in Blue* for his 1924 Aeolian Hall concert. The *Pittsburgh Post* of January 16, 1923, noted that Whiteman played "weird near-human concoctions before a gold-encrusted curtain, and later in front of a patent leather forest inhabited by black and white beauties," referring to the costumes of the chorus girls.

DOLORES COSTELLO (1903–1979), C. 1923. Pittsburgh-born Dolores Costello began her career in the *Scandals* as a dancer with the "George White Girls." Her first edition was 1922, and she appeared in two other Gershwin-scored versions, in 1923 and 1924. Dolores and her father Maurice were both silent-film actors, with Dolores appearing from childhood in nearly 50 silents as well as in many early talkies. Her most notable later role was in Orson Welles's *The Magnificent Ambersons.* Married to legendary actor John Barrymore, she was the grandmother of Drew Barrymore. (Library of Congress Prints and Photographs Division and Alfred Cheney Johnson.)

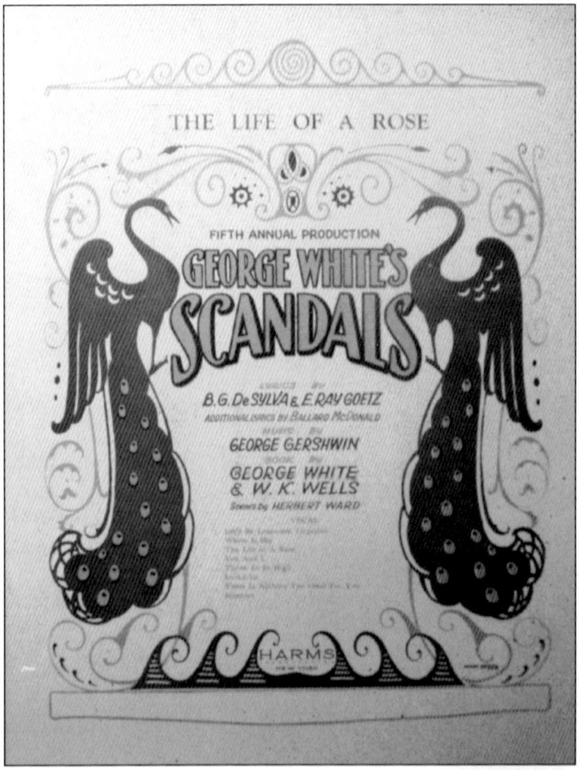

SHEET MUSIC FOR THE SCANDALS OF 1923. Gershwin's "The Life of a Rose" was part of the *Scandals*' fifth annual edition (in Pittsburgh at the Nixon Theatre in January 1924). *Scandals* music was composed to accompany the show's individual themed sections, such as a human-roses pageant with this song. Similarly, mechanical dolls and a Pullman-train scene were supported, respectively, by Gershwin's "Little Scandal Doll" and "Where Is She?"

PROMOTIONAL HANDBILL FOR *GEORGE WHITE'S SCANDALS*. These general advertising heralds/handbills could be utilized for various road-tour productions. This one for the Columbia Theatre in San Francisco proclaims, "This massive production exactly as presented for one solid year at the Apollo Theatre in New York is coming intact in 3 special baggage cars—same wonderful Parisian costumes & draperies, same numerous comedy scenes, same marvelous novelty effects, and the famous George White Beauties."

Nixon Theatre Postcard. The Nixon Theatre was the stopover home for all five of Gershwin's editions of *George White's Scandals*, which seemed to appear there magically in January of the year following the Broadway version. The ornate Pittsburgh showplace seated about 2,200. It closed in 1950 (its name was used at another location on Liberty Avenue thereafter), when it was razed and replaced by the Alcoa Building.

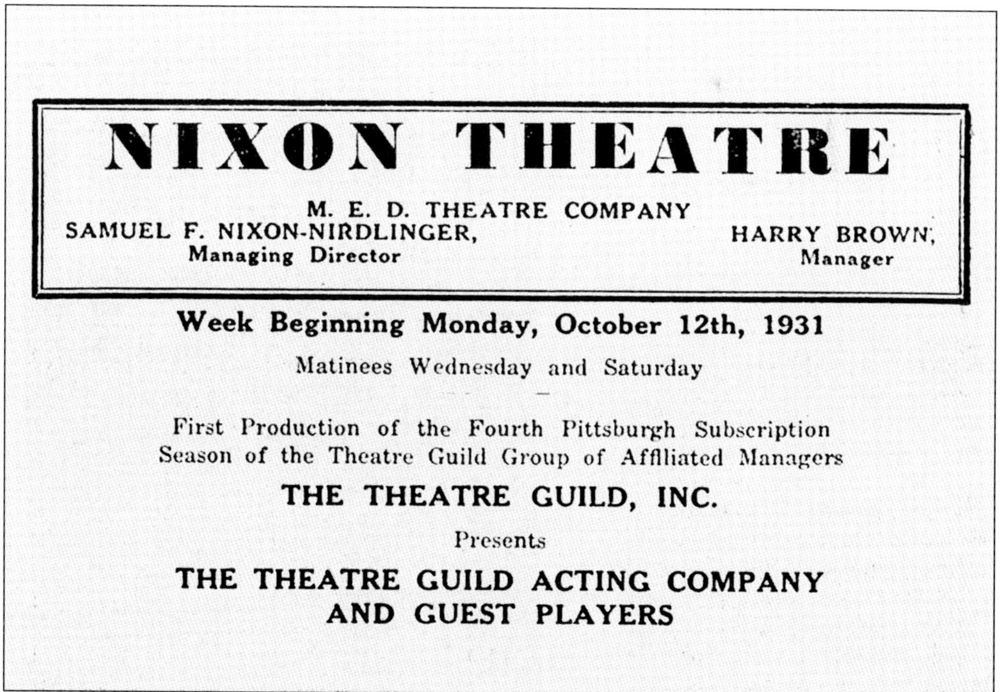

NIXON THEATRE

M. E. D. THEATRE COMPANY

SAMUEL F. NIXON-NIRDLINGER, Managing Director

HARRY BROWN, Manager

Week Beginning Monday, October 12th, 1931

Matinees Wednesday and Saturday

First Production of the Fourth Pittsburgh Subscription Season of the Theatre Guild Group of Affiliated Managers

THE THEATRE GUILD, INC.

Presents

THE THEATRE GUILD ACTING COMPANY AND GUEST PLAYERS

Nixon Theatre Program. This typical Nixon program page introduces a road-tour tryout presentation for October 1931. It was produced by the Theatre Guild, which would bring Gershwin's *Porgy and Bess* to Pittsburgh in 1936.

SHEET MUSIC FOR THE *SCANDALS* OF *1924*. The sixth annual edition, the last of Gershwin's *Scandals*, played in Pittsburgh at the Nixon Theatre in January 1925. There were two different cover designs for the 1924 *Scandals*. This version for "Somebody Loves Me" spotlights one of George White's chorines, Dorothy Sebastian, whose alluring poses decorate many *Scandals* publicity advertisements and handbills. The song had prominent exposure in such films as 1945's *Rhapsody in Blue* and 1952's *Somebody Loves Me* and, from the beginning, has been one of Gershwin's most recorded tunes, a favorite of jazz musicians.

WINNIE LIGHTNER (1899–1971). Lightner was a comedian-singer who performed in three Gershwin-scored editions of *George White's Scandals*. She was acclaimed for introducing "Somebody Loves Me" in 1924's *Scandals*. Lightner was also featured in many early-sound movie musicals, including *Gold Diggers of Broadway*, *The Show of Shows*, *Hold Everything*, and *Manhattan Parade*.

Five

The Classic Gershwin Musicals on Tour

The early song-interpolation revues and musicals and *Scandals* paved the way for many other Gershwin shows—ones for which he wrote the complete scores—to stop in Pittsburgh during their pre- and post-Broadway road tours. Some shows were not successful and closed in New York, or out of town, after a minimal number of performances (*Half Past Eight* of 1919, *Strike Up the Band* of 1927, *Treasure Girl* of 1928, *Pardon My English* of 1933), and some only traveled to a few select cities, such as Boston, Philadelphia, Chicago, and San Francisco. Others were created specifically for British audiences (*The Rainbow*, *Primrose*). Yet, many did get to the Steel City after their New York runs, with performances at the Alvin and Nixon Theatres. Among these major Gershwin gems are *La La Lucille*, *Sweet Little Devil*, *Lady, Be Good!*, *Tell Me More*, *Oh, Kay!*, and *Rosalie*.

La La Lucille was Gershwin's first successful complete musical comedy; a post–New York tour brought it to the Nixon on February 9, 1920. Sheet music for almost all the songs (14, with a few unused) popularized the music, with notable hits being "Tee-Oodle-Um-Bum-Bo" (also for a piano roll played by Gershwin himself) and the haunting "Nobody but You."

Lady, Be Good! brought its original stars, the inimitable dancing/comedy/singing duo of Fred and Adele Astaire, as did *Rosalie* (with New York lead Marilyn Miller). Both were smash hits. *Oh, Kay!*'s darling of two continents, Gertrude Lawrence, was garnering raves in London for her performance in the show's British iteration; Pittsburgh (at the Alvin in February 1928) instead enjoyed Julia Sanderson as the lead.

Sweet Little Devil and *Tell Me More* are today lesser-known shows, but their music is top-notch Gershwin. They played in Pittsburgh, respectively, at the Alvin in October 1924 and at the Nixon in September 1925. *Girl Crazy* had a major stage production at the Loew's Penn movie theater in 1932.

As for *Of Thee I Sing*—a show with Pittsburgh native George S. Kaufman sharing author credits with Morrie Ryskind—after 441 performances on Broadway, this Pulitzer Prize–winning operetta toured the nation for about eight months, arriving at the Nixon Theatre in March 1933.

GEORGE GERSHWIN, C. 1926. Gershwin traveled to London to prepare the British *Lady, Be Good!* production in 1926, and this may be an aboard-ship photograph from that trip. (Library of Congress Prints and Photographs Division.)

PROMOTIONAL HANDBILL FOR *LA LA LUCILLE* ROAD TOUR. *La La Lucille* of 1919 was Gershwin's first successful complete show; a post–New York tour brought it to the Nixon Theatre in February 1920. It received favorable reviews for both its story and music, despite the composer being almost unknown to the critics (this was before his "Swanee" fame). In retrospect, "Nobody but You" is the standout ballad from this show and a favorite of Gershwin, who used it for a piano variation/transcription in his 1932 *Song-Book*.

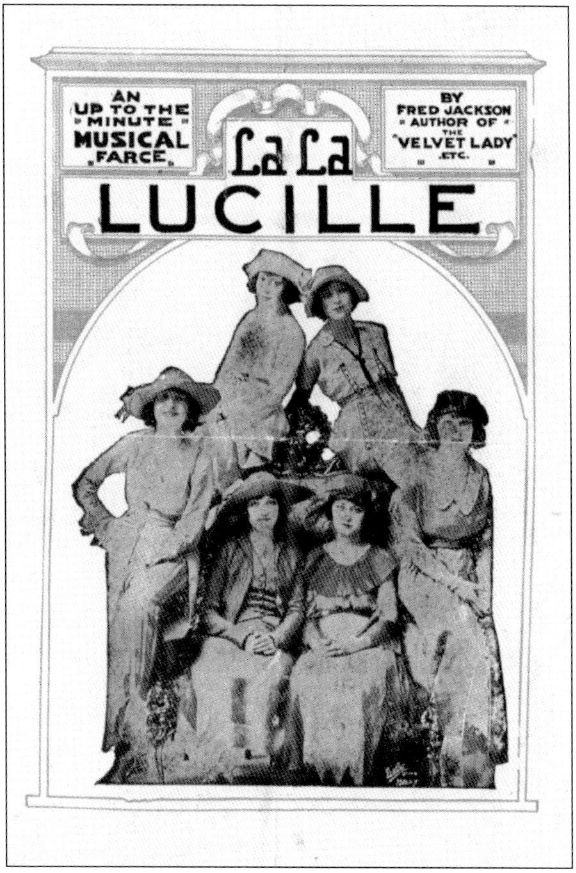

BOX LABEL FOR THE PIANO ROLL OF "TEE-OODLE-UM-BUM-BO." This audience favorite from Gershwin's *La La Lucille* (May–August 1919 in New York) was played on a piano roll by its composer. Gershwin frequently produced such rolls for both his own and others' pieces during his early performing years in order to augment his income.

PROMOTIONAL HANDBILL FOR *LADY, BE GOOD!* ROAD TOUR. *Lady, Be Good!* was the first complete show with the Gershwin brothers writing as a team and Ira credited under his own name. Featuring the brother-and-sister dancers Fred and Adele Astaire, it was a huge success and marked the recognition of George Gershwin as an innovative "jazz" composer of musical shows. "Fascinating Rhythm" and "Oh, Lady Be Good!" were just two of the songs that gained contemporary—and lasting—fame. *Lady, Be Good!* (tour handbill's cover and interior shown here) came to Pittsburgh's Nixon Theatre in October 1925.

FRED (1899–1987) AND ADELE (1896–1981) ASTAIRE IN *LADY, BE GOOD!*, 1924. In *The Art of Stage Dancing* (1925), Pittsburgh-born Ned Wayburn wrote, "Two of my most famous pupils in musical comedy dancing are Fred and Adele Astaire. . . . I was able to place them in vaudeville in a singing and dancing act, which I had prepared for them. This started them on their career, which has led them to Europe and back again. . . . Now they are starring in *Lady, Be Good,* on tour after a long run in New York." Gershwin traveled with the Astaires to London with the show, adding two new songs there: "Buy a Little Button" and "I'd Rather Charleston." This photograph (from *Play Pictorial*, 1926) is from the "Swiss Miss" number in the British production.

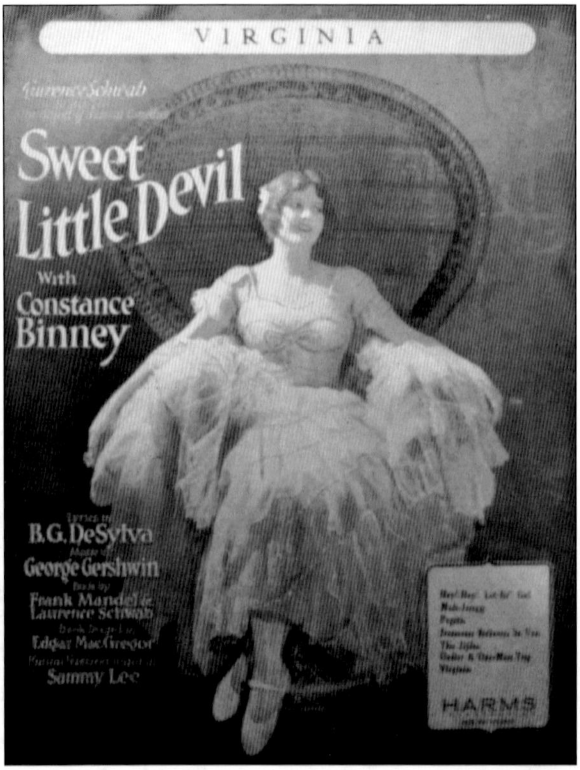

SHEET MUSIC FOR *SWEET LITTLE DEVIL*, 1924. Like so many of the 1920s shows, *Sweet Little Devil* was built around a specific stage personality—in this case, Constance Binney (pictured on this cover). Binney portrayed the character reflected in this song's title of "Virginia." Originally called *A Perfect Lady*, this *Devil* teased audiences at Pittsburgh's Alvin Theatre in October 1924.

SHEET MUSIC FOR *OH, LADY! LADY!!*, 1918. Broadway's *Oh, Lady! Lady!!* arrived at Pittsburgh's Alvin Theatre in February 1919. While not a Gershwin show, almost all the participants in the production were involved in Gershwin's early rise to fame. Jerome Kern, a personal hero of Gershwin who was the composer of *Miss 1917*, wrote the music; P.G. Wodehouse (who would co-write lyrics for the Gershwins' *Oh, Kay!* and *Rosalie*) supplied the lyrics; and Guy Bolton (future co-writer of the Gershwins' *Lady, Be Good!* and *Girl Crazy*) developed the story. Both Vivienne Segal (*Miss 1917*, *A Dangerous Maid*) and Constance Binney (*Sweet Little Devil*) were featured players.

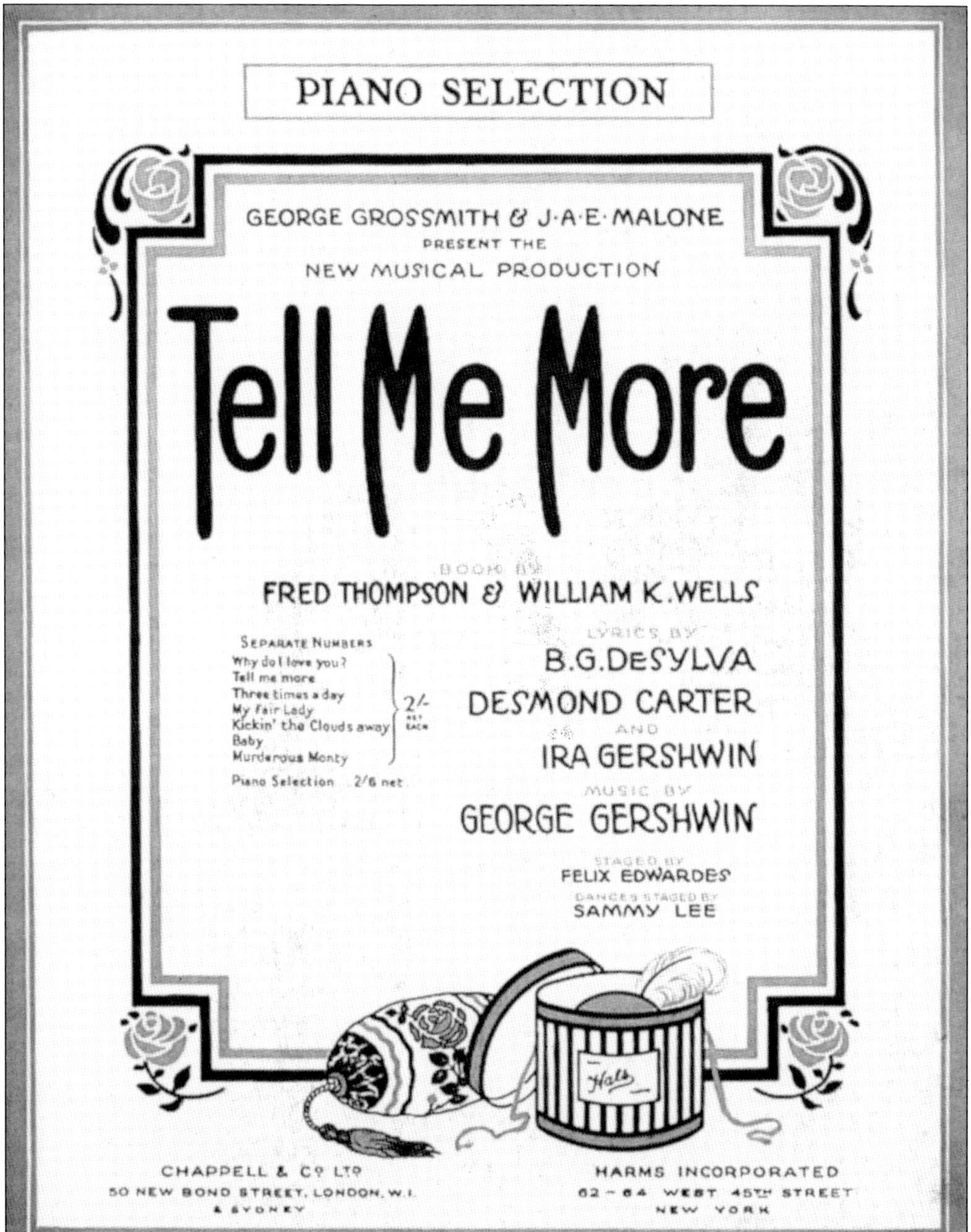

SHEET MUSIC FOR *TELL ME MORE*, 1925. This lesser-known Gershwin show had some of his most complex and interesting numbers to date. The US touring production visited Pittsburgh at the Nixon in September 1925. This music sheet is from the London production. The earliest version of the show was called *My Fair Lady* (with premature apologies to Lerner and Loewe) and had its tryout at the Nixon Theatre in Atlantic City.

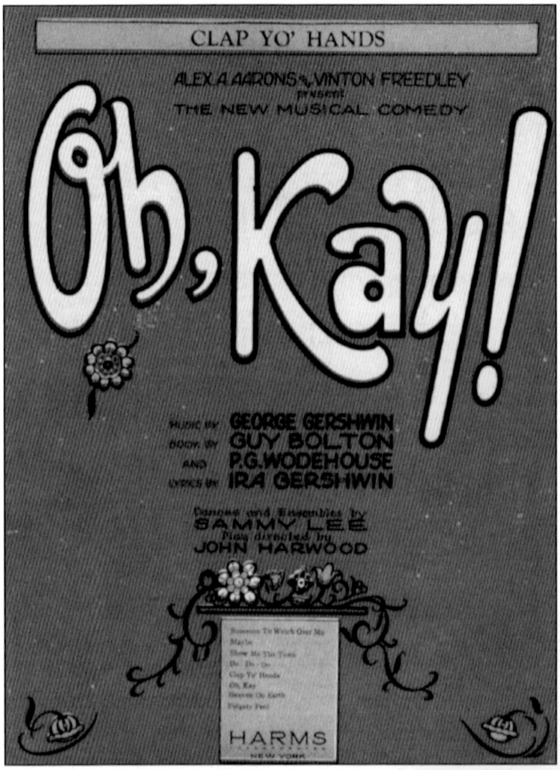

Sheet Music for *Oh, Kay!*, 1926. This was one of Gershwin's most popular musicals, containing such perennial favorites as "Maybe," "Do, Do, Do," and "Someone to Watch Over Me." Ira Gershwin was only able to partly complete his lyric-writing duties due to a hospital stay, so Howard Dietz supplied the words for several songs. After a smash-hit London stop, *Oh, Kay!* toured the United States and played at the Alvin in February 1928.

Gertrude Lawrence (1898–1952). *Oh, Kay!* was a vehicle for George Gershwin's good friend Gertrude Lawrence, who would later star in his *Treasure Girl*—badly reviewed and basically unsuccessful, but with such song gems as "I've Got a Crush on You"—and in a 1944 Ira Gershwin show with music by Kurt Weill, *Lady in the Dark*. Lawrence was idolized for her *Oh, Kay!* role in both New York and London. For the road tour that reached Pittsburgh in early 1928, she was replaced by Julia Sanderson. (Billy Rose Theatre Division, the New York Public Library.)

NIXON THEATRE ADVERTISEMENT FOR *ROSALIE*, 1928. This playbill advertisement heralded an upcoming Gershwin show, *Rosalie*, set for the Nixon Theatre. This production with Marilyn Miller played in Pittsburgh November–December 1928. Though two songs were singled out by reviewers (and recording artists)—"Say So!" and "Oh Gee! Oh Joy!"—it was "How Long Has This Been Going On?" that would achieve lasting fame. (Curtis Theatre Collection, Hillman Library, University of Pittsburgh.)

MARILYN MILLER (1898–1936). *Rosalie* was a lavish 1928 Ziegfeld show starring Marilyn Miller, one of the period's great female theater performers. Miller was yet another talented woman Gershwin had encountered while playing piano for the *Ziegfeld Follies of 1918*. *Rosalie*, even as a musical collaboration with Sigmund Romberg, became one of George Gershwin's great successes. The legendary Joseph Urban designed the sets; shortly afterward, he created the Urban Room at Pittsburgh's William Penn Hotel.

PLAYBILL ADVERTISEMENT FOR *GIRL CRAZY*, 1930. One of the Gershwins' biggest successes, this musical introduced the immortal "I Got Rhythm," made Ethel Merman and Ginger Rogers stars, and featured an all-star jazz pit band with Benny Goodman, Jack Teagarden, Jimmy Dorsey, Glenn Miller, and Gene Krupa. In Pittsburgh, a version of the show played in May 1932 at the Loew's Penn movie theater. Oddly enough, at about the same time, the 1932 movie of *Girl Crazy* was showing at Pittsburgh's Warner.

PITTSBURGH'S LOEW'S PENN THEATRE, 1937. One of Pittsburgh's great movie theaters, the Loew's and United Artists Penn stood at the corner of Sixth Street and Fort Duquesne Boulevard. Newspaper publicity in May 1932 proclaimed, "Loew's Penn for the first time in its history will present a complete musical comedy on the stage, opening Friday—*Girl Crazy* by George Gershwin" (*Pittsburgh Sun-Telegraph*), with the *Pittsburgh Press* adding, "A musical show of this size is a decided innovation in motion picture theater entertainment." Today, the building is the opulent Heinz Hall. (Pittsburgh City Photographer Collection, University of Pittsburgh.)

SHEET MUSIC FOR *OF THEE I SING*, 1931. The Gershwins' longest-running show was a collaboration with Pittsburgher George S. Kaufman. After well over a year on Broadway and winning a Pulitzer Prize, *Of Thee I Sing* was ready to travel and arrived at the Nixon Theatre in March 1933.

Six

A Rhapsody and Blue Laws

The more "serious" musical events in Pittsburgh were held at the Syria Mosque, a venue dating from 1916. Three of Gershwin's concert performances were there: the famous Paul Whiteman "Experiment in Modern Music" that had introduced Gershwin's *Rhapsody in Blue* at Aeolian Hall in Manhattan, the 1933 Pittsburgh Symphony concert with Gershwin as special guest to inaugurate Sunday performances and end the blue laws, and the 1934 *Rhapsody in Blue* anniversary national tour with the Leo Reisman Orchestra.

Besides utilizing these Pittsburgh locations, Gershwin continued his connection to the city through his friends and associates. The Whiteman concert, for example, included a commissioned work by Victor Herbert, who had previously been conductor of the Pittsburgh Symphony. Pittsburgh native Oscar Levant hosted Gershwin's train ride west and evening post-concert event at the home of Bertha Rauh. Her offer came to Gershwin via another Pittsburgh associate, George S. Kaufman.

For the Whiteman-Gershwin-*Rhapsody* tour, the newly tagged "Experiment in American Music" was presented at Pittsburgh's Syria Mosque on Saturday afternoon and evening, May 17, 1924. Gershwin, who was pianist in his *Rhapsody* for much of the tour, including Pittsburgh, left after the performance in St. Louis on May 21 to return to New York and work on the music for the 1924 *Scandals*.

In 1933, Gershwin revisited the three-rivers city to perform as soloist in a special "end of the blue laws" concert by the Pittsburgh Symphony on November 19. A lengthy article in the *Pittsburgh Post-Gazette* on November 20, 1933, offered an account of the event at the Syria Mosque, stating that the sold-out concert represented "the largest crowd ever to attend a symphony concert" there.

In a July 15, 1937, *Pittsburgh Post-Gazette* article taking note of Gershwin's passing ("Pittburghesque"), Charles R. Danver gave some intriguing details about that evening:

> There was a buffet supper [at the Rauh residence] and afterwards Gershwin and Levant headed for the music room. Then began one of the most exciting piano recitals the guests had ever heard. Modern music, jazz, played by its two outstanding masters. First the composer of the *Rhapsody in Blue* played; then Levant played, and finally the two sat down together and turned out one duet after another. And so, far into the night. A good time was had by all—except the Rauh grand piano, which took a terrible beating. It was discovered later that the pianists had broken four of the keys!

GEORGE GERSHWIN, LATE 1920S. This publicity photograph of the composer was used for many theatrical/concert programs. (Library of Congress Prints and Photographs Division.)

Promotional Handbill for Paul Whiteman's Aeolian Hall "Experiment in Modern Music," 1924. For his modern-music concert, Paul Whiteman decided to commission a concert work from George Gershwin based on their collaboration on the "Stairway to Paradise" number (and *Blue Monday* mini-opera) in George White's *Scandals of 1922* and also owing to Gershwin's growing reputation as a "serious" (and jazzy) composer of popular songs, as demonstrated by his performance with Eva Gauthier at her November 1923 recital at Aeolian Hall. The result was, of course, *Rhapsody in Blue.*

"Experiment in Modern Music" Program. The startling unveiling of *Rhapsody in Blue* with Gershwin as pianist enlivened the crowd near the end of Paul Whiteman's February 12, 1924, concert, which aimed to equate jazz/popular music with the classics. Pieces by Victor Herbert, Zez Confrey, and Rudolf Friml were part of the effort to bridge the gap, and Gershwin's *Rhapsody* sealed the deal, with a tumultuous reaction by the audience and then appreciative reviews for the new direction in music and the young composer.

Sheet Music for *Rhapsody in Blue*, 1924. Gershwin's *Rhapsody* was written, in a matter of weeks, especially for Paul Whiteman's "Modern Music" concert—after Ira Gershwin read a newspaper notice about the bandleader's plans. It quickly brought its composer international fame and influenced the musical styles of many famous musicians. This is the original version for two pianos.

FERDE GROFÉ (1892–1972). A composer and arranger for the Paul Whiteman Orchestra, Grofé helped Gershwin finish the orchestration for *Rhapsody in Blue* so he could have the commissioned work ready for Whiteman in time for the February 12, 1924, concert. Grofé went on to compose, inspired by symphonic jazz and Gershwin, many orchestral works in that vein, such as the *Grand Canyon Suite*, *Metropolis*, *Mississippi Suite*, and more.

VICTOR HERBERT (1859–1924). One of America's great operetta composers (*The Red Mill*, *Babes in Toyland*), Victor Herbert was invited by Whiteman to contribute a work to the "Experiment in Modern Music," resulting in *A Suite of Serenades*. During rehearsals, Herbert offered Gershwin some suggestions for the *Rhapsody*, which Gershwin gratefully adopted. Herbert appears here due to his association with the Pittsburgh Symphony, as its conductor from 1898 to 1904. (Library of Congress Prints and Photographs Division.)

WHITEMAN'S "EXPERIMENT" AT PITTSBURGH'S SYRIA MOSQUE, 1924. In the weeks following the famous Aeolian Hall concert in New York, Whiteman and Gershwin (who, by this time, merited mention on the program cover) toured with the slightly renamed "Experiment in American Music." A brief article in the *Pittsburgh Sun* on the day of the concert announced that "Whiteman arrived this morning" for two concerts at the Syria Mosque and that the tour thus far had been playing to "capacity audiences." Gershwin was pianist in his *Rhapsody* for many of the tour stops, including in Pittsburgh at the Syria Mosque on May 17, 1924. Gershwin left the tour after the performance in St. Louis later in May. (Curtis Theatre Collection, Hillman Library, University of Pittsburgh.)

THE WHITEMAN "EXPERIMENT" TOUR *CONCERT BULLETIN*. This September 27, 1924, program booklet spotlighting the Whiteman concert was already featuring reviews from tour-city newspapers, including this one from the *Pittsburgh Gazette Times*: "Yesterday Pittsburgh heard for the first time the quite original and decidedly bizarre orchestra developed and conducted by Paul Whiteman. . . . Whiteman is credited with accomplishing more in the direction of better development of jazz through his orchestra concerts than any other man living."

Syria Mosque and the Pittsburgh Symphony. The Syria Mosque was built by the Shriners, who dedicated their first Pittsburgh temple in 1902. A new and larger facility was opened in October 1916 in the city's Oakland neighborhood, home to the University of Pittsburgh. The structure at the time was characterized as having "Moorish revival features" and had the largest concert hall in Pittsburgh. John Phillip Sousa and his band frequently appeared here from 1917 through 1924. Victor Herbert directed the Pittsburgh Symphony from 1898 to 1904. Paul Whiteman's "Experiment in American Music," highlighted by George Gershwin performing his *Rhapsody in Blue*, came to the Syria Mosque in May 1924. Due to financial problems, the Pittsburgh Symphony Orchestra (PSO) disbanded in 1909 but was revived in 1926, resuming its concert series at the Syria Mosque. Ironically, the first concert of the new PSO on Sunday, April 24, 1926, at the Syria Mosque defied Pittsburgh's blue laws (playing non-religious music on a Sunday)—and nine symphony board members were arrested. During Antonio Modarelli's 1930s tenure as conductor, George Gershwin was invited to perform at the symphony's first legal Sunday concert after the abolition of the Pennsylvania blue laws. (Edward J. Shourek Photograph Collection, University of Pittsburgh.)

KING OF JAZZ WINDOW CARD, 1930. Pittsburgh movie theaters such as the Stanley and the Warner inevitably screened numerous movies associated with Gershwin. Of interest because of its historical status, *King of Jazz* is a filmed Paul Whiteman revue, with lavish sets, early Technicolor, a Walter Lantz cartoon, and *Rhapsody in Blue* (unfortunately minus Gershwin) as the spectacle's centerpiece.

PITTSBURGH'S STANLEY THEATRE, 1928. Just a few years after its 1928 opening, this elegant Steel City movie palace ran newspaper advertisements in June 1930 for its screenings of *King of Jazz*. Located on Seventh Street and Penn Avenue, in 1987 the Stanley became one of modern Pittsburgh's great concert/theatrical venues, the Benedum Center for the Performing Arts.

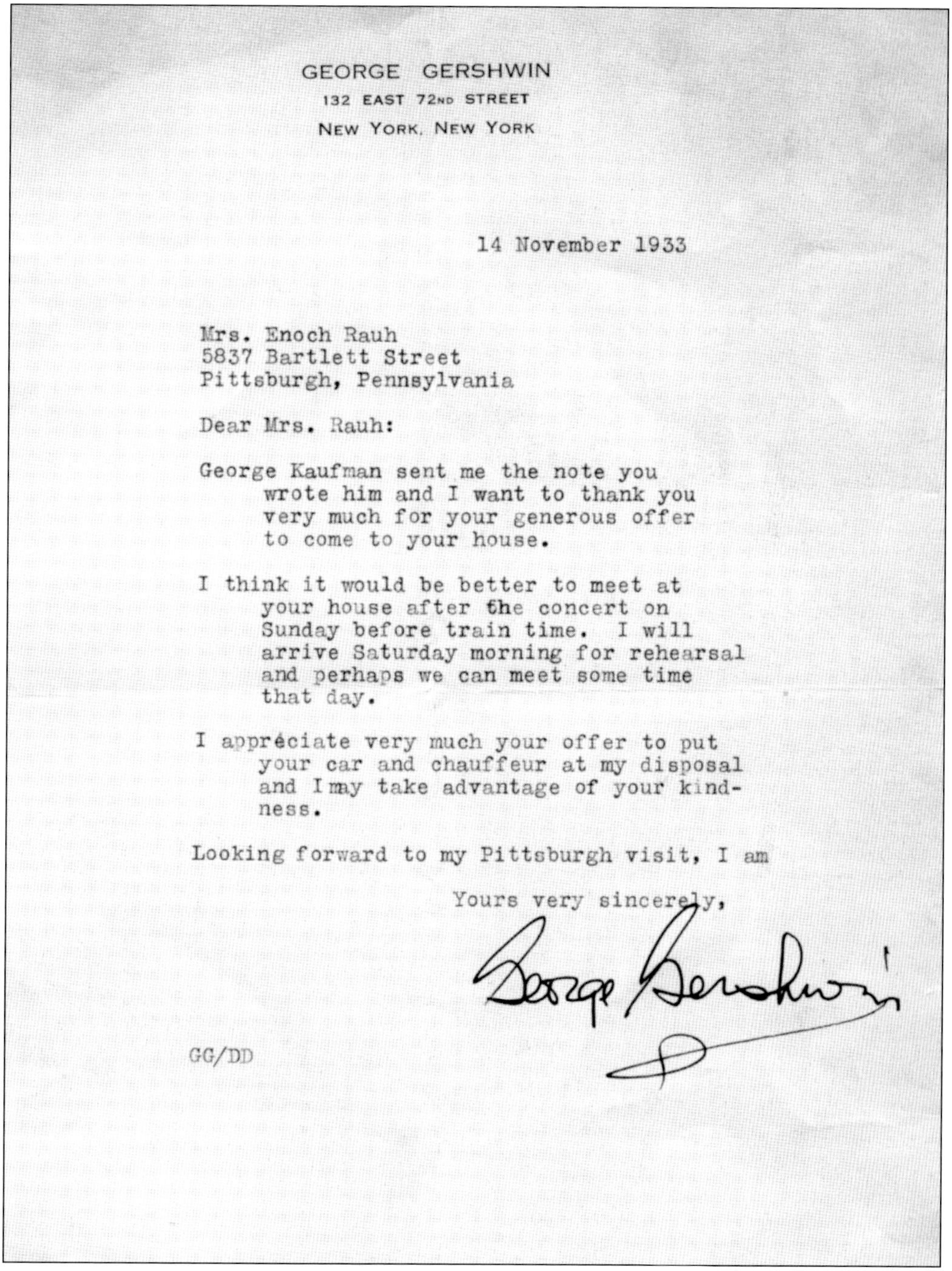

GEORGE GERSHWIN
132 EAST 72ND STREET
NEW YORK, NEW YORK

14 November 1933

Mrs. Enoch Rauh
5837 Bartlett Street
Pittsburgh, Pennsylvania

Dear Mrs. Rauh:

George Kaufman sent me the note you wrote him and I want to thank you very much for your generous offer to come to your house.

I think it would be better to meet at your house after the concert on Sunday before train time. I will arrive Saturday morning for rehearsal and perhaps we can meet some time that day.

I apprécíate very much your offer to put your car and chauffeur at my disposal and I my take advantage of your kindness.

Looking forward to my Pittsburgh visit, I am

Yours very sincerely,

George Gershwin

GG/DD

LETTER FROM GEORGE GERSHWIN, 1933. This letter dated November 14, 1933, from Gershwin to his potential host, Bertha Rauh (1865–1952), head of the city's Department of Public Welfare, accepts an invitation to visit for the evening after his 1933 concert with the Pittsburgh Symphony. This was a response to an intermediary effort by Pittsburgh's George S. Kaufman, playwright and collaborator on many Gershwin musicals. The composer writes, "I think it would be better to meet at your house after the concert on Sunday before train time." (Richard E. Rauh Family Papers, Rauh Jewish Archives, Heinz History Center.)

GERSHWIN WELCOMED IN PITTSBURGH FOR THE 1933 BLUE LAWS CONCERT. Gershwin visited Pittsburgh to inaugurate the Symphony Society's Sunday concerts. This newspaper photograph from November 20, 1933, is of the ceremony preceding the composer's November 19 performance at the Syria Mosque. The accompanying article reported of the sold-out concert, "Gershwin himself made Pennsylvania history on the steps of the Mosque yesterday afternoon, selling the first ticket—first for the concert and first ever legally sold for a Sunday concert in the state." The article also noted Gershwin's comments before the newsreel cameras: " 'I consider it a great honor to be able to sell the first ticket ever sold in Pittsburgh for a Sunday concert. Although I like blue music, I can't say I'm very fond of Blue Laws,' he said. . . . 'I'm certainly glad I'm in Pittsburgh for this occasion. . . . I always like to be around when new things happen and especially when anything is as epoch-making as this concert.' " (Pittsburgh Symphony Orchestra and the Rauh Jewish Archives, Heinz History Center.)

GERSHWIN'S 1933 PITTSBURGH SYMPHONY CONCERT PROGRAM. Gershwin made several symphony-orchestra guest appearances in the Midwest. Future Pittsburgh Symphony conductor Fritz Reiner invited him to perform with the Cincinnati Symphony Orchestra in March 1927, and he played three of his serious works with the Chicago Symphony Orchestra on June 14, 1933. A few months later, he was in Pittsburgh to inaugurate Sunday concerts in Pennsylvania, with the revocation of the blue laws.

RECORDING OF AN AMERICAN IN PARIS, 1929. *An American in Paris* was performed in the second half of the 1933 Pittsburgh Symphony's blue laws concert, which also featured the *Concerto in F* and *Rhapsody in Blue*. Pictured here is the label of the 1929 Victor 78rpm record; the piece was conducted by Nathaniel Shilkret and supervised by Gershwin, who played the celesta part.

WILLIAM DALY (1887–1936). Gershwin's friend and musical advisor Bill Daly conducted many Gershwin stage shows and concerts, including the 1933 Pittsburgh Symphony blue laws event at the Syria Mosque. Daly also conducted the *Scandals of 1924*, *Tip-Toes*, *Oh, Kay!*, the failed 1927 version of *Strike Up the Band*, *Show Girl*, and *Let 'Em Eat Cake*; the 1931 and 1932 Lewisohn Stadium concerts with the New York Philharmonic; and Gershwin's appearance in June 1933 with the Chicago Symphony.

Oscar Levant, Gershwin's 1933 Guide to Pittsburgh. By this time, Pittsburgh-born Oscar Levant was an essential part of Gershwin's circle. In *A Smattering of Ignorance*, Levant discussed his role in the 1933 visit, which occasioned one of the notorious wit's most famous stories about his friend: "It was through my professional association with George that I made my re-entry into Pittsburgh musical life . . . when Gershwin was invited to play the *Rhapsody* and *Concerto* with the orchestra there. . . . So George suggested that I come out with him and play the solo parts while he got the orchestra in shape." The two shared a drawing room during the overnight train trip and discussed music before settling in for the night, with Gershwin claiming the lower berth. "I adjusted myself to the inconveniences of the upper berth," Levant wrote. "At this moment my light must have disturbed George's doze, for he opened his eyes, looked up at me and said drowsily, 'Upper berth—lower berth. That's the difference between talent and genius.' "

Pittsburgh's William Penn Hotel, 1935. After a long evening of partying and concertizing at the Rauh home following the Syria Mosque performance, Gershwin and Levant missed their train back to New York. Thus, they had to stay overnight at a city hotel. Research at the William Penn Hotel has confirmed Gershwin's stay there the night of the concert. The hotel opened in 1916 and after 1928 underwent renovations, which added a ballroom—the Art Deco Urban Room, created by Joseph Urban, the greatest set designer for Jazz Age Broadway shows (and the Metropolitan Opera), including *Rosalie* and other Gershwin musicals. (Pittsburgh City Photographer Collection, University of Pittsburgh.)

Seven

Of Kaufman, an Anniversary Tour, and Radio Days

The years 1933 and 1934 represented a very productive Gershwin-in-Pittsburgh period, with 1933 marking the composer's guest appearance at the Pittsburgh Symphony's blue laws concert. It was also the year when the touring company of Gershwin's most successful and popular theater work, *Of Thee I Sing* (a musically complex operetta that won a Pulitzer Prize), played in Pittsburgh at the Nixon for over a week in March 1933.

Besides his brother Ira and co-author Morrie Ryskind, Gershwin's collaborator in this endeavor was playwright George S. Kaufman. Pittsburgh-born Kaufman worked with George and Ira Gershwin and Morrie Ryskind to create a trilogy of groundbreaking political-satire operettas: *Strike Up the Band*, *Of Thee I Sing*, and *Let 'Em Eat Cake*. Kaufman did not direct the Pittsburgh version of *Of Thee I Sing*, as he had done in New York, and his only stage return as director to his native city seems to have been for *Once in a Lifetime* (at the Alvin in October 1931). But most other Kaufman plays did reach the Steel City; a version of *Dulcy*, for example, was produced at the Alvin in 1922 and by the Pitt Players in 1926.

In early 1934, Gershwin embarked on what was billed as a "Tour Celebrating the Tenth Anniversary of *Rhapsody in Blue*," with the Leo Reisman Orchestra (Charles Previn conducted in place of an incapacitated Reisman) and operatic singer James Melton. It was during these concerts that Gershwin introduced a new symphonic work, the *"I Got Rhythm" Variations*.

The performance in Pittsburgh was at the Syria Mosque on Tuesday, February 6, 1934. The following day, the *Pittsburgh Press* printed a laudatory review by music critic Ralph Lewando: "Gershwin disclosed virtuosic command of the keyboard, and he was recalled again and again to acknowledge the sustained applause which he generously shared with his musicians and conductor."

As soon as the anniversary tour was finished in February 1934, Gershwin embarked on a year-long stint as a radio host—in part to help finance (with $2,000 weekly checks) his opera *Porgy and Bess*, on which he was concurrently working.

Music by Gershwin was heard on two different national networks, in both 15-minute and half-hour formats, and was well publicized. The series, which ended on December 23, 1934, was heard in Pittsburgh on KDKA.

GEORGE GERSHWIN, **1934.** This portrait graced the souvenir program for the composer's "Tenth Anniversary of the *Rhapsody in Blue*" national tour.

OF THEE I SING ROAD TOUR SOUVENIR PROGRAM, 1933. In the early 1930s, George S. Kaufman—with George and Ira Gershwin and Morrie Ryskind—created a trilogy of groundbreaking political-satire operettas: *Strike Up the Band*, *Of Thee I Sing*, and *Let 'Em Eat Cake*. *Of Thee I Sing* was the biggest hit of all the Gershwin brothers' musicals, and won a 1932 Pulitzer Prize for Kaufman and his writing cohorts (George's music—the most complex and ambitious score of all his musicals—was ineligible). The operetta ran for 441 performances on Broadway, with a simultaneous national tour starting in September 1932. For the touring version, the principal actors were replaced with Oscar Shaw, Donald Meek, Cecil Lean, and Harriette Lake—better known as film and television star Ann Sothern. It reached Pittsburgh's Nixon Theatre in March 1933.

George S. Kaufman (1889–1961). Unlike Oscar Levant, Kaufman was not drawn back to his home city, only returning occasionally for tour productions of his plays. Still, Pittsburgh's Alvin and Nixon Theatres hosted the visits of Kaufman's famous stage works, such as *Dulcy*, *You Can't Take It with You*, and *Once in a Lifetime*. Kaufman usually collaborated with co-writers Marc Connelly, Moss Hart, and Morrie Ryskind. He worked with Ira Gershwin on the lyrics for 1924's *Be Yourself* and then collaborated with Ryskind and the Gershwins on *Of Thee I Sing* and two other satiric operettas. (Billy Rose Theatre Division, the New York Public Library.)

Scene from *Of Thee I Sing*, 1931. This scene from the New York production includes the show's original lead actors (from left to right at center), Lois Moran, Victor Moore, and William Gaxton. After its road tour, the musical returned to Broadway for another month in spring 1933. (Billy Rose Theatre Division, the New York Public Library.)

Tour Celebrating the Tenth Anniversary
of "Rhapsody in Blue"

PRESENTING

GEORGE GERSHWIN

Composer - Pianist

JAMES MELTON, *Tenor*

and the

REISMAN SYMPHONIC ORCHESTRA

CHARLES PREVIN, *Conductor*

In a Program of Gershwin Successes

SPRINGFIELD AUDITORIUM

WEDNESDAY, JANUARY 17, 1934

THE 1934 *RHAPSODY IN BLUE* ANNIVERSARY TOUR PROGRAMS. For Gershwin's multicity "Tenth Anniversary of the *Rhapsody in Blue*" concert tour with the Leo Reisman Orchestra, tenor James Melton provided the vocal elements, and Charles Previn conducted in place of the ailing Reisman. The performance at the Syria Mosque took place on Tuesday, February 6, 1934. Music critic Ralph Lewando noted in the *Pittsburgh Press* Gershwin's "virtuosic command of the keyboard."

Rhapsody in Blue

Concerto in F

American in Paris

"——— to be true music and lasting, music must repeat the thoughts and aspirations of the people and the times. My people are Americans. My time is today."
GEO. GERSHWIN

Gershwin Hits:
"Swanee"
"Man I Love"
"I Got Rhythm"
Music for 5 "Scandals"
"Lady, Be Good"
"Oh Kay"
"Tip Toes"
"Funny Face"
"Girl Crazy"
"Of Thee I Sing" (Pulitzer Prize Winner)
"Let 'Em Eat Cake" (New on Broadway)
And next season "Porgy" in Opera produced by the Theatre Guild

GEORGE GERSHWIN

with his fabulous gift for writing has to his credit more successful musical comedies and song hits than any three other contemporaries combined.

His music is danced to by smart young America, whistled by the street urchin and sung in "blues" and "rhythms" by musical comedy queens, and played by the great symphony orchestras of America and Europe. When he sits at the piano and plays his own numbers, the effect that he evokes is extraordinary.

Each decade has its own particular idol in music, and Gershwin is the favorite of today.

CHARLES PREVIN will direct the Leo Reisman Symphonic Orchestra on Mr. Gershwin's tour.

A favorite leader on Broadway, he has conducted innumerable musical comedy successes, starting with Mr. Gershwin's "La La Lucille", and more recently his greatest hit—"Of Thee I Sing".

JAMES MELTON

internationally known tenor of radio and concert stage, will be the soloist with Mr. Gershwin.

He has been voted the most popular singer on the air both as soloist and with the Revelers Quartet, here and in Europe.

A Southerner, Melton's collegiate musical activities began with his playing the saxophone in orchestras, and in the Glee Clubs of the Universities of Florida and Georgia; later he attended Vanderbilt University. His success in New York and many of the great Eastern cities has been phenomenal.

Syria Mosque Postcards. Pittsburgh's Syria Mosque was a concert venue for symphonic events, such as the Gershwin appearances with the Paul Whiteman Orchestra in 1924, the Pittsburgh Symphony in 1933, and the Leo Reisman Orchestra in 1934. From 1930 to 1937, Antonio Modarelli (from nearby Braddock, Pennsylvania) was the PSO's director. Other music directors thereafter—performing at the Syria Mosque until 1971, when the PSO moved to its current home at Heinz Hall—were Otto Klemperer, Fritz Reiner, and William Steinberg.

Charles Previn (1888–1973). A conductor for several Gershwin shows (*La La Lucille*, *Of Thee I Sing*, Ira's *Two Little Girls in Blue*) and concerts, Previn visited the Steel City for the *Rhapsody* anniversary tour. The *Pittsburgh Press* review on February 7, 1934, headlined "Gershwin and His Tunes Thrill 2,000 in Concert," noted that Previn conducted without a score or baton. Charles Previn was a relative of André Previn, musical director of the Pittsburgh Symphony Orchestra from 1976 through 1984.

James Melton (1904–1961). For the "Tenth Anniversary of the *Rhapsody in Blue*" concerts, opera singer James Melton sang traditional/folk songs as well as some Gershwin tunes. Ralph Lowando in the *Pittsburgh Press* noted that Melton's "voice is of luscious quality throughout its wide compass." Melton was known as a singer of both popular and operatic music, performing in radio, movies, and—in the 1940s—at the Metropolitan Opera.

Leo Reisman (1897–1961). It was the Leo Reisman Orchestra that accompanied George Gershwin on his 1934 tour, but it lacked Leo due to an accident that waylaid him. Charles Previn stepped in as guest conductor. Reisman also merits a place in Pittsburgh musical and radio history since, according to Fadograph's Weblog, his was probably the first band to perform live on the city's KDKA (or KQV) radio in the early 1920s. Reisman was also inspired by Whiteman's Aeolian Hall concert to stage a similar "symphonic jazz" event in February 1928 in Boston with compositions by W.C. Handy, Ferde Grofé, and Charles Martin Loeffler. During World War II, Reisman, with Victor Borge at the piano, regularly performed *Rhapsody in Blue* for several months at the Waldorf Wedgewood Room in New York.

SHEET MUSIC FOR "FASCINATING RHYTHM." This "fascinating" piece from *Lady, Be Good!* was one of the songs for piano that Gershwin played as his finale in the anniversary concert. Originally titled "Syncopated City," the song broke new musical ground for the Gershwin brothers, with its insistent rhythmic patterns and jazz-mad lyric. The sheet music shown is from *Lady, Be Good!*'s British production.

SHEET MUSIC FOR "THE MAN I LOVE." Another anniversary-concert piano piece, "The Man I Love" was not from a show but was an international signature piece perennially looking for a stage home (this sheet music was for an attempt to place it in *Strike Up the Band*). Both "Fascinating Rhythm" and "The Man I Love" (popularized in its orphaned form by Helen Morgan) are 1924 compositions. It is probable for this concert that Gershwin played his special piano-transcription versions based on his 1932 *Song-Book*.

GEORGE GERSHWIN

Born Brooklyn, Sept. 26, 1898. From a piano-pounding song plugger at $15 per week to a world-famous composer, who has elevated jazz to classical heights—that's George Gershwin's accomplishment. A few years ago he was razzed so unmercifully by an unappreciative audience at Fox's City Theatre in New York that he dashed out of the place without collecting his paycheck. Twelve years later, the Fox Company paid him $50,000 for the rights to let Paul Whiteman play his "Rhapsody in Blue." His compositions range from musical comedy numbers to concertos for symphony orchestras.

Gershwin on the Radio. Shown are two printed notices relating to Gershwin's year as host of his own radio program, *Music by Gershwin*, in 1934. The top item appeared in *The Blue Book of Radio Entertainers* in 1935. The magazine page's photograph below shows Gershwin at the microphone during a program. *Music by Gershwin* was broadcast in Pittsburgh on KDKA. On another Pittsburgh station, WJAS, he was heard as a guest on the *Waring's Pennsylvanians* show on February 25, 1934.

THE STORY OF GEORGE GERSHWIN

(Continued from page 7)

actual piano lessons as a foundation.

At 15, he knew that he wanted to be a professional musician. A year later found him working as a song-plugger for J. H. Remick and Company, at $15 a week.

Eight to 10 hours a day, George plugged.

"I'll gamble on you," he said. "I'll give you $35 a week without any set duties. Just step in every morning, so to speak, and say 'Hello.' The rest will follow." George thought so, too.

Thus, before he was 20, Gershwin was

his marked liking for strong, interesting basses.

He wrote the music for five of George White's Scandals, and he wrote the music of the Pulitzer Prize-winning play, "Of Thee I Sing."

Eight

A Grand Jazz Opera

Writing a grand opera had been on Gershwin's mind since the 1920s. *Porgy* was first a novel by DuBose Heyward, which Gershwin had read in 1926. *Porgy* the play was produced in New York by the Theatre Guild to great acclaim in 1927, and played in Pittsburgh in both January and November 1929. Heyward and Gershwin signed a contract with the Theatre Guild in October 1933 to create an opera to be named *Porgy and Bess*. The guild announced its new project, and Heyward mailed the first working pages of the opera to Gershwin in the same week as Gershwin's Pittsburgh travels for his blue laws appearance with the Pittsburgh Symphony. Thus, the birth of *Porgy and Bess* is forever linked to Gershwin's involvement with the Steel City.

After a critically successful opening in Boston, the Theatre Guild presented *Porgy and Bess* at the Alvin Theatre in New York, starting October 10, 1935. It ran for 124 performances. The opera's road tour began in late January 1936 and included Philadelphia, Pittsburgh, Chicago, and Washington, DC, where it closed in March. *Porgy and Bess* opened at the Nixon Theatre in Pittsburgh for a weeklong run commencing February 10, 1936.

Rouben Mamoulian was the opera's director in New York and for the tour. He left this portrait of Gershwin (quoted in Merle Armitage's *George Gershwin*, 1938):

> George was so completely naive and innocent in his liking of his own work that it actually became one of the endearing qualities of his nature. . . . I remember once I had to meet George and several other friends for dinner. . . . I was late so I went there unshaven and rather haggard-looking. I apologized to the company for my appearance. George said, "Rouben, don't apologize. Personally, I love you when you're unshaven." "Why, George?" I asked. "Because," said he, "when you're unshaven you look like me."

The reception given his opera in Pittsburgh certainly must have warmed Gershwin's heart. Ralph Lewando wrote in the *Pittsburgh Press*, "Here, indeed, is something new—new in idiom, new in musical treatment, and new in subject matter for the lyric theater. . . . We might term it a new accent on opera." Lewando's colleague in the drama seat, Kaspar Monahan, chimed in: "As an opera . . . *Porgy and Bess* is the best I've ever witnessed from the standpoint of acting combined with music."

George Gershwin, mid-1930s. This photograph shows Gershwin at the piano, composing and notating at the time of *Porgy and Bess*. (Library of Congress Prints and Photographs Division.)

Porgy and Bess Program, 1935. Gershwin began sporadic work on *Porgy and Bess* a little before a January 1934 visit to his librettist, DuBose Heyward, in South Carolina. The composing was interrupted by his *Rhapsody* anniversary tour, which lasted through early February 1934. He worked on the opera despite hosting the *Music by Gershwin* radio show for the rest of the year. The Theatre Guild presented *Porgy and Bess* at the Alvin Theatre in New York starting October 10, 1935.

Rouben Mamoulian (1897–1987). One of the most innovative directors of Hollywood's Golden Age (*Love Me Tonight*, *Dr. Jekyll and Mr. Hyde*, *Silk Stockings*, *Applause*—the last with Helen Morgan, who popularized Gershwin's "The Man I Love"), Rouben Mamoulian directed the Pittsburgh and other tour performances of *Porgy and Bess*, as he had done in New York for the Theatre Guild's *Porgy* (1927) and the 1935 opera. For Otto Preminger's 1959 movie of *Porgy and Bess*, Mamoulian directed several segments, most unused.

Eva Jessye (1895–1992). Eva Jessye founded her chorus in 1926 and quickly established it as the preeminent vocal organization specializing in spirituals, African American folk music, and classical works. In 1934, the Eva Jessye Choir triumphed in one of the seminal modern American operas, *Four Saints in Three Acts* by Virgil Thomson and Gertrude Stein. For 1935's *Porgy and Bess*, Gershwin himself engaged the Eva Jessye Choir, which was heard in the Pittsburgh productions of *Porgy and Bess* in 1936 and 1943.

J. Rosamond Johnson (1873–1954). Johnson brothers J. Rosamond and James Weldon were prominent musical figures during the Harlem Renaissance. Rosamond is best known as the composer of "Lift Every Voice and Sing," while also writing many other songs and arranging spirituals and theater music from 1900 through the 1920s. Also an actor, he performed the role of Lawyer Frazier in *Porgy and Bess* in 1935. (Van Vechten Collection, Library of Congress Prints and Photographs Division.)

Anne Brown (1912–2009). Brown was a classically trained, Juilliard-educated singer who had just graduated when she wrote to Gershwin asking for an audition for his upcoming opera. She ended up assisting and advising the composer as the composition progressed—and was gratified when he offered her the main female role of Bess. Brown continued as Bess when the opera came to Pittsburgh in 1936.

Scene from *Porgy and Bess*, 1935. This panoramic scene from the 1935 Theatre Guild production of *Porgy and Bess* in New York shows the massing and architectural distribution of figures on the stage, for which director Rouben Mamoulian was well known. (US Farm Security Administration/Office of War Information, Library of Congress Prints and Photographs Division.)

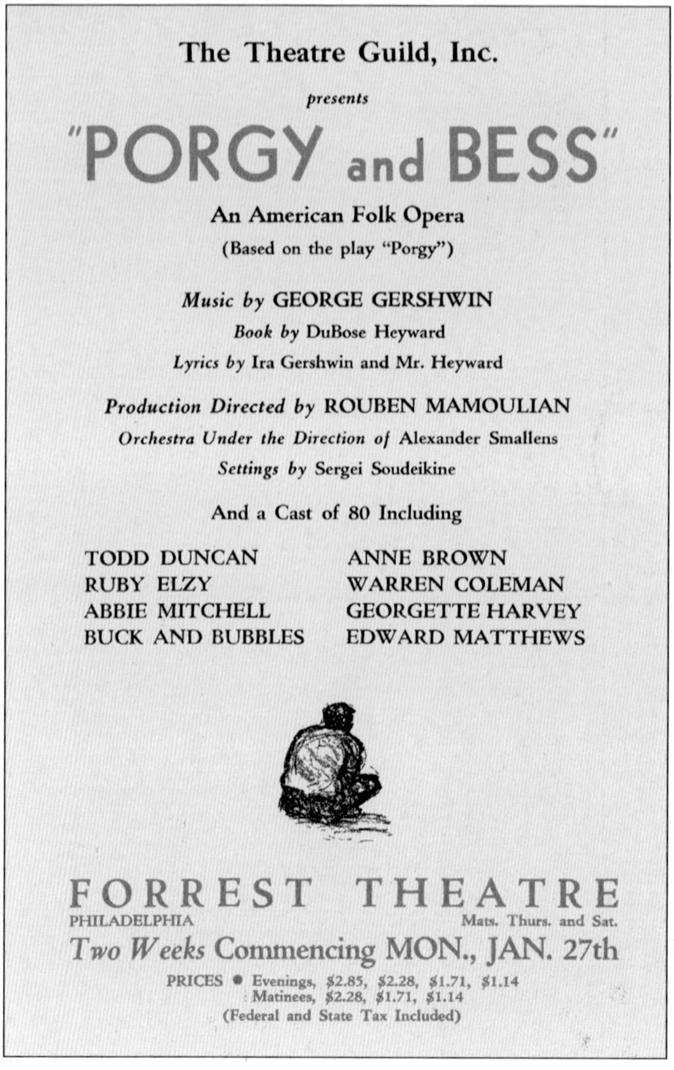

The Theatre Guild, Inc.

presents

"PORGY and BESS"

An American Folk Opera

(Based on the play "Porgy")

Music by GEORGE GERSHWIN

Book by DuBose Heyward

Lyrics by Ira Gershwin and Mr. Heyward

Production Directed by ROUBEN MAMOULIAN

Orchestra Under the Direction of Alexander Smallens

Settings by Sergei Soudeikine

And a Cast of 80 Including

TODD DUNCAN — ANNE BROWN
RUBY ELZY — WARREN COLEMAN
ABBIE MITCHELL — GEORGETTE HARVEY
BUCK AND BUBBLES — EDWARD MATTHEWS

FORREST THEATRE

PHILADELPHIA — Mats. Thurs. and Sat.

Two Weeks Commencing MON., JAN. 27th

PRICES • Evenings, $2.85, $2.28, $1.71, $1.14
Matinees, $2.28, $1.71, $1.14
(Federal and State Tax Included)

Porgy and Bess Road Tour Program. This handbill program is for the opera's presentation at the Forrest Theatre in Philadelphia, similar to Pittsburgh's in February 1936. The opera's brief road tour (January through March 1936) also included stays in Chicago and Washington, DC.

Porgy and Bess at the Nixon Theatre, 1936. Pictured is the Nixon's *Porgy and Bess* cast-and-credits handbill for the week beginning February 10, 1936. After the somewhat lukewarm reaction by New York critics, Gershwin must have been gratified by the reception given his opera in Pittsburgh. Ralph Lewando's review in the *Pittsburgh Press* on February 11, 1936, characterized *Porgy and Bess* as "new in idiom, new in musical treatment, and new in subject matter for the lyric theater."

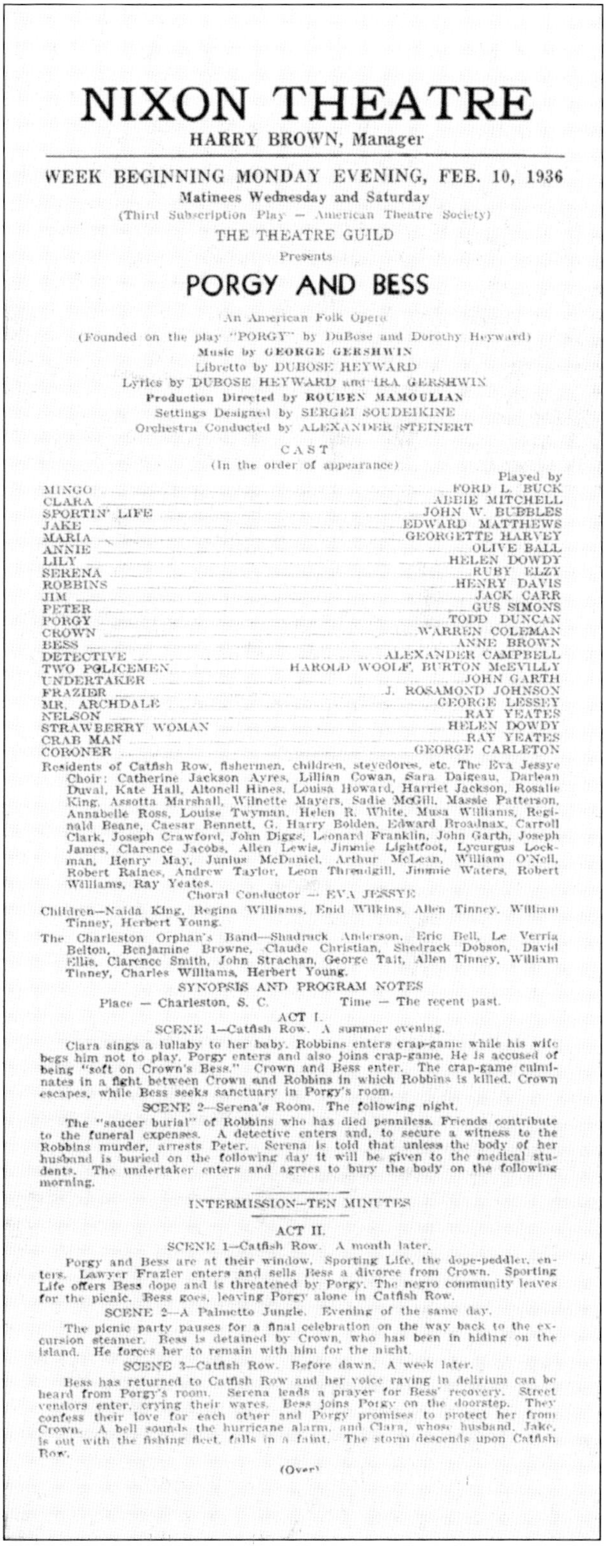

NIXON THEATRE

HARRY BROWN, Manager

WEEK BEGINNING MONDAY EVENING, FEB. 10, 1936

Matinees Wednesday and Saturday

(Third Subscription Play — American Theatre Society)

THE THEATRE GUILD

Presents

PORGY AND BESS

An American Folk Opera

(Founded on the play "PORGY" by DuBose and Dorothy Heyward)

Music by GEORGE GERSHWIN

Libretto by DUBOSE HEYWARD

Lyrics by DUBOSE HEYWARD and IRA GERSHWIN

Production Directed by ROUBEN MAMOULIAN

Settings Designed by SERGEI SOUDEIKINE

Orchestra Conducted by ALEXANDER STEINERT

CAST

(In the order of appearance)

	Played by
MINGO	FORD L. BUCK
CLARA	ABBIE MITCHELL
SPORTIN' LIFE	JOHN W. BUBBLES
JAKE	EDWARD MATTHEWS
MARIA	GEORGETTE HARVEY
ANNIE	OLIVE BALL
LILY	HELEN DOWDY
SERENA	RUBY ELZY
ROBBINS	HENRY DAVIS
JIM	JACK CARR
PETER	GUS SIMONS
PORGY	TODD DUNCAN
CROWN	WARREN COLEMAN
BESS	ANNE BROWN
DETECTIVE	ALEXANDER CAMPBELL
TWO POLICEMEN	HAROLD WOOLF, BURTON McEVILLY
UNDERTAKER	JOHN GARTH
FRAZIER	J. ROSAMOND JOHNSON
MR. ARCHDALE	GEORGE LESSEY
NELSON	RAY YEATES
STRAWBERRY WOMAN	HELEN DOWDY
CRAB MAN	RAY YEATES
CORONER	GEORGE CARLETON

Residents of Catfish Row, fishermen, children, stevedores, etc. The Eva Jessye Choir: Catherine Jackson Ayres, Lillian Cowan, Sara Daigeau, Darlean Duval, Kate Hall, Altonell Hines, Louisa Howard, Harriet Jackson, Rosalie King, Assotta Marshall, Wilnette Mayers, Sadie McGill, Massie Patterson, Annabelle Ross, Louise Twyman, Helen R. White, Musa Williams, Reginald Beane, Caesar Bennett, G. Harry Bolden, Edward Broadnax, Carroll Clark, Joseph Crawford, John Diggs, Leonard Franklin, John Garth, Joseph James, Clarence Jacobs, Allen Lewis, Jimmie Lightfoot, Lycurgus Lockman, Henry May, Junius McDaniel, Arthur McLean, William O'Neil, Robert Raines, Andrew Taylor, Leon Threadgill, Jimmie Waters, Robert Williams, Ray Yeates.

Choral Conductor — EVA JESSYE

Children—Naida King, Regina Williams, Enid Wilkins, Allen Tinney, William Tinney, Herbert Young.

The Charleston Orphan's Band—Shadrack Anderson, Eric Bell, Le Verria Belton, Benjamine Browne, Claude Christian, Shedrack Dobson, David Ellis, Clarence Smith, John Strachan, George Tait, Allen Tinney, William Tinney, Charles Williams, Herbert Young.

SYNOPSIS AND PROGRAM NOTES

Place — Charleston, S. C. Time — The recent past.

ACT I.

SCENE 1—Catfish Row. A summer evening.

Clara sings a lullaby to her baby. Robbins enters crap-game while his wife begs him not to play. Porgy enters and also joins crap-game. He is accused of being "soft on Crown's Bess." Crown and Bess enter. The crap-game culminates in a fight between Crown and Robbins in which Robbins is killed. Crown escapes, while Bess seeks sanctuary in Porgy's room.

SCENE 2—Serena's Room. The following night.

The "saucer burial" of Robbins who has died penniless. Friends contribute to the funeral expenses. A detective enters and, to secure a witness to the Robbins murder, arrests Peter. Serena is told that unless the body of her husband is buried on the following day it will be given to the medical students. The undertaker enters and agrees to bury the body on the following morning.

INTERMISSION—TEN MINUTES

ACT II.

SCENE 1—Catfish Row. A month later.

Porgy and Bess are at their window. Sporting Life, the dope-peddler, enters. Lawyer Frazier enters and sells Bess a divorce from Crown. Sporting Life offers Bess dope and is threatened by Porgy. The negro community leaves for the picnic. Bess goes, leaving Porgy alone in Catfish Row.

SCENE 2—A Palmetto Jungle. Evening of the same day.

The picnic party pauses for a final celebration on the way back to the excursion steamer. Bess is detained by Crown, who has been in hiding on the island. He forces her to remain with him for the night.

SCENE 3—Catfish Row. Before dawn. A week later.

Bess has returned to Catfish Row and her voice raving in delirium can be heard from Porgy's room. Serena leads a prayer for Bess' recovery. Street vendors enter, crying their wares. Bess joins Porgy on the doorstep. They confess their love for each other and Porgy promises to protect her from Crown. A bell sounds the hurricane alarm, and Clara, whose husband, Jake, is out with the fishing fleet, falls in a faint. The storm descends upon Catfish Row.

(Over)

George Gershwin

George Gershwin, whose "Porgy and Bess" has been hailed by no less an authority than Sergei Koussevitsky, conductor of the Boston Symphony Orchestra, as the "first real American opera," has long been one of America's most distinguished popular composers and now, with his latest work, takes high rank among the nations composers of serious music.

He was born in Brooklyn and in his youth took no particular interest in music. As a matter of fact, he considered those of his playmates who took music lessons "sissies." However, when his family acquired a second-hand piano the keys fascinated him and, after developing a somewhat sheepish interest in the instrument, he asked for a teacher. He had several—for he learned so rapidly that he wore his instructors out. The last of these, Charles Hambitzer, succeeded in inculcating in the youth a genuine interest in music and his influence was perhaps the most important in Gershwin's musical life.

Working diligently, Gershwin became an accomplished pianist but his early use of his talent was not exactly promising. His debut in the field of music was in Tin Pan Alley, as a lowly song-plugger at a wage of only $15 a week. It was while he was thus employed that he sold his first composition—a song which went for a song, for it brought him only $5. He continued to write melodies and came to the attention of Max Dreyfus, who employed him on the composing staff of Harms, Inc., music publishers, at $35 a week.

Gershwin lived up to Mr. Dreyfus' belief in him and eventually was given his first real opportunity to do a full musical score. It was for a musical comedy called "La La Lucille!" He continued to write for the musical comedy stage, doing work for several of George White's "Scandals" and other shows. But it was a song fashioned independently that developed into his first real hit.

Porgy and Bess Souvenir Program, 1935. A beautifully designed 24-page booklet celebrated the opera during its New York run. In addition to lists of the cast, scenes, and musical numbers, it featured essays on how the opera was created, a story synopsis, and many stage photographs. Shown is the page with Gershwin's biography.

Nine

A Hollywood Year

As he was creating his theatrical and concert masterworks, George Gershwin had a parallel career getting his music into Hollywood films. Some silent films actually adapted his stage plays, with some of his songs played live in accompaniment; for *The Sunshine Trail* of 1923, he and his brother wrote a theme song. When talkies came along, his *Rhapsody in Blue* was the centerpiece of the ballyhooed color musical revue *King of Jazz*, featuring Paul Whiteman with his orchestra—a film that played in Pittsburgh at the Stanley Theatre. *Delicious* for Fox was Gershwin's first original score, which included a shortened version of his *New York Rhapsody* (written in full for the film and which later emerged as his *Second Rhapsody*).

The brief Gershwin Hollywood golden age, however, lasted but a year, after the brothers moved to California in 1936 and just as the *Suite from Porgy and Bess*, Gershwin's last original concert work, was making the national rounds. The Gershwins worked on three Hollywood scores, two of which George did not live to see in their motion-picture formats.

Gershwin was contracted by RKO Pictures for two films that would reunite him with his old friend Fred Astaire; *Shall We Dance* and *A Damsel in Distress* were both released in 1937. Even in Hollywood, Gershwin maintained his Pittsburgh connection, for the head of production on these two movies (as well as on a long list of other notable films, both musical and dramatic) was Pandro S. Berman, from the Steel City. *Shall We Dance* is the masterpiece of these last three films, with its background music, ballet piano music, the famous "Walking the Dog" instrumental sequences, and a long ballet finale, not to mention such immortal songs as "They Can't Take That Away from Me," "They All Laughed," and "Let's Call the Whole Thing Off."

Gershwin tragically died on July 11, 1937, before completing work on his last film for Sam Goldwyn (who was to produce the 1959 movie of *Porgy and Bess*). Nevertheless, *The Goldwyn Follies* includes the Gershwin standards "Love Walked In" and "Love Is Here to Stay" and features another famous movie star from Pittsburgh: Adolphe Menjou.

George Gershwin in Hollywood. This c. 1936 photograph captures Gershwin during the period of his last three film scores. (Library of Congress Prints and Photographs Division.)

Sheet Music for *The Sunshine Trail*, 1923, and Scene from *Girl Crazy*, 1932. Two unsung but significant beginnings to George Gershwin's film-music career were *The Sunshine Trail* (Thomas H. Ince Corp.) and *Girl Crazy* (RKO Radio Pictures). For the former, Gershwin wrote a silent-movie theme song with his brother Ira (as Arthur Francis). For the movie *Girl Crazy*, based on the Gershwin show, he was asked to add another original tune, "You've Got What Gets Me." *Girl Crazy* played in Pittsburgh at the Warner Theatre, among others, in mid-April 1932. (Below, Museum of Modern Art Film Stills Archive.)

ADVERTISEMENT FOR *DELICIOUS*, 1931. Gershwin's first Hollywood assignment was for the Janet Gaynor film *Delicious*. His score includes several songs, an operetta-like "Dream Sequence," and a reduced version of his then-new symphonic work, *Second Rhapsody*. The movie's advertisements prominently mention and picture Gershwin. *Delicious* (Fox Film Corp.) played at Pittsburgh's Fulton Theatre in early January 1932 (the Fulton became the prestigious Byham Theater in 1991).

Scene from *Delicious*. This scene depicts the various ethnic passengers on a ship bringing immigrants to America, with Janet Gaynor at center. Later in the film, Gaynor's character wanders through a shadowy, surrealistic montage of New York impressions, underscored by Gershwin's new rhapsody. (Museum of Modern Art Film Stills Archive.)

***Delicious* Creative Team.** This photograph of Gershwin (with brother Ira as lyricist, along with screenwriter Guy Bolton) was part of a large and gorgeous color advertisement for *Delicious* published in the 1932 Fox Corp. annual promotional pressbook.

Shall We Dance Poster, 1937. *Shall We Dance* (RKO Radio Pictures) is the best of Gershwin's last three films, due to the many instrumental gems scattered throughout—from ballet music to the famous "Walking the Dog" sequences scored by Gershwin—and to such now-classic songs as "They Can't Take That Away from Me," "They All Laughed," and "Let's Call the Whole Thing Off."

Fred Astaire and Ginger Rogers in *Shall We Dance*. This is the famous roller-skating sequence in the film. The two stars dance on skates to the music of the Gershwin song "They All Laughed." The image appeared as part of a 1937 RKO advertising series in *Film Daily*.

Scene from *Shall We Dance*. This masterful Art Deco composition is the setting for the grand finale of the film, with Fred Astaire and Harriet Hoctor initially dancing in ballet style and then morphing into a jazzy culmination with Fred and Ginger reunited to the orchestral variations of Gershwin's song "Shall We Dance." (Museum of Modern Art Film Stills Archive.)

Movie Herald Advertisement for *Shall We Dance*. Steel City moviegoers were able to enjoy the Gershwin-scored *Shall We Dance* at the Loew's United Artists Penn Theatre in 1937. Kaspar Monahan's *Pittsburgh Press* review on May 15, 1937, was headlined, "Astaire and Rogers Score Once Again in *Shall We Dance* at Loew's Penn."

Harriet Hoctor (1905–1977), 1920. Harriet Hoctor, seen in this photograph by Edward Thayer Monroe, was acknowledged for her performances straddling the worlds of ballet and popular dance. She had been the featured dancer in the *American in Paris Ballet* section of the Gershwin musical *Show Girl*. *Shall We Dance*'s extended ballet/dance finale represents the movie's theme of two dance worlds and even has several different moods of music. Astaire starts out in a ballet with Hoctor ("Hoctor's Ballet") and finally reclaims Rogers as his jazz partner at the conclusion of the "Shall We Dance Ballet."

Pandro S. Berman (1905–1996). Even in Hollywood, Gershwin maintained his Pittsburgh connection. The head of production on his two RKO movies, *Shall We Dance* and *A Damsel in Distress*, was Pandro S. Berman from the Steel City. Berman was one of the greatest of all Hollywood producers; working for RKO, he paired Fred Astaire with Ginger Rogers for eight films, guided the early career of Katharine Hepburn, and distributed Disney animation, including the groundbreaking *Snow White and the Seven Dwarfs*.

Advertisement for *A Damsel in Distress*, 1937. A Fred Astaire film without Ginger Rogers, *A Damsel in Distress* (RKO Radio Pictures) nevertheless contains some of George Gershwin's finest songs, from "Nice Work If You Can Get It" to "A Foggy Day (in London Town)"—and even two English madrigal-type songs in keeping with the British setting. The story was adapted from a novel by P.G. Wodehouse, a familiar name from Gershwin stage shows.

SCENE FROM *A DAMSEL IN DISTRESS*. The famed comedy team of Burns and Allen provides the energy and a great deal of the dancing in *Damsel*, serving as Fred Astaire's primary partners since Joan Fontaine—not much of a dancer—had replaced Ginger Rogers as Fred's love interest. Astaire and George Burns and Gracie Allen more than compensate with two long and inventive sequences—the most notable being a funhouse extravaganza—to Gershwin's "Stiff Upper Lip" and "Put Me to the Test." (Museum of Modern Art Film Stills Archive.)

MOVIE HERALD ADVERTISEMENT FOR *A DAMSEL IN DISTRESS*. The film opened in downtown Pittsburgh at the Loew's Penn on December 10, 1937, and then moved on to the city's Enright and Sheridan Square movie theaters in January and February. Movie heralds were small, cheap handouts that announced upcoming movies for particular theaters.

THE *GOLDWYN FOLLIES* LOBBY CARD, 1938. Gershwin tragically died on July 11, 1937, before completing work on his last film, *The Goldwyn Follies* (1938), for Sam Goldwyn, who later produced the 1959 movie of *Porgy and Bess*. Still, this *Follies* (Samuel Goldwyn Co.) is known for offering the timeless Gershwin tunes "Love Walked In" and "Love Is Here to Stay." Pittsburgh was represented by the renowned character actor Adolphe Menjou. The score was completed by Ira with Vernon Duke. In the film, another Gershwin song, "I Was Doing All Right," is heard briefly on the radio, sung by Ella Logan. Gershwin was to have composed a new ballet for Vera Zorina and her choreographer husband, George Balanchine. When Gershwin passed away before writing this sequence, Balanchine proposed (and constructed) an *American in Paris* ballet, but Goldwyn rejected that in favor of two new ballet compositions by Vernon Duke: the *Romeo and Juliet* and *Water Nymph* ballets.

Adolphe Menjou (1890–1963). A featured player in Gershwin's final movie, *The Goldwyn Follies*, Pittsburgh's Adolphe Menjou by this time had already had a long movie career, dating back to the silents, notably in Charlie Chaplin's 1923 *A Woman of Paris*. Among his nearly 150 films from the 1910s through the 1950s were *The Front Page*, *Gold Diggers of 1935*, *A Star Is Born*, *Stage Door*, *You Were Never Lovelier*, *State of the Union*, *The Hucksters*, and *Paths of Glory*.

Helen Jepson (1904–1997). Also appearing in *The Goldwyn Follies* was Helen Jepson, famed Metropolitan Opera soprano and radio star. Born in Titusville, Pennsylvania—about 80 miles north of Pittsburgh—Jepson, together with opera star Lawrence Tibbett, made the first recording of music from *Porgy and Bess*, with Alexander Smallens conducting. That 1935 Victor 78rpm album includes the proclamation that it was "recorded under the supervision of the composer."

Ten

ENCORE

The importance of Pittsburgh for Gershwin and his music did not end with the composer's tragic passing in July 1937. His Pittsburgh associates continued his legacy.

Robert Russell Bennett, Gershwin's orchestrator for many of his shows and films, produced *Porgy and Bess: A Symphonic Picture* for the 1943 season of the Pittsburgh Symphony; it was commissioned by the PSO's musical director, Fritz Reiner.

Reiner enjoyed a lifelong association with Gershwin and his music. Gershwin was piano soloist at a Cincinnati Symphony Orchestra concert conducted by Reiner in March 1927. Reiner conducted part of a 1931 Lewisohn Stadium all-American concert with Gershwin's music. Later, in 1939 and 1941, Reiner conducted the Pittsburgh Symphony Orchestra in Gershwin compositions, as interpreted by Oscar Levant.

It was Levant who most prominently promoted Gershwin's music, often doing so in his native Pittsburgh. Levant had helped Gershwin rehearse the two-piano versions of many of his major concert works, and beginning in 1932, played Gershwin's music at the Lewisohn Stadium concerts, including the memorial All-Gershwin Program on July 10, 1939. With Reiner's Pittsburgh Symphony, Levant played the *Concerto in F* and conducted the premiere of his own composition, *Dirge* ("In Memory of George Gershwin"), in November 1939. He returned as soloist with the Symphony in 1941, 1947, and 1950.

Oscar Levant appeared in a number of movies, usually portraying a wisecracking pianist. In Hollywood's version of Gershwin's life, *Rhapsody in Blue* (1945), Levant played himself.

It was left to another Pittsburgh son, Gene Kelly, to produce the ultimate homage to George Gershwin. In the 1930s, Kelly directed the University of Pittsburgh's annual Cap and Gown Club productions. To create one of the greatest of all movie musicals, 1951's *An American in Paris*, Kelly scooped up a huge amount of Gershwin music. With his major role in the film, Oscar Levant was once again in the spotlight shining from the spirit of George Gershwin.

Maxine Sullivan, from neighboring Homestead, Pennsylvania, was a renowned jazz vocalist who gained wide praise for her renditions of Gershwin songs at the 1938 Gershwin memorial concert at New York's Lewisohn Stadium. Another Pittsburgher, classical pianist Earl Wild, spent much of his career performing and recording (and writing variations on) Gershwin's music.

Other singers and musicians with Pittsburgh associations who have played a part in the Gershwin story over the decades include Lena Horne, Helen Jepson, Lorin Maazel, André Previn, and Marvin Hamlisch.

GEORGE GERSHWIN BY CARL VAN VECHTEN. Gershwin seems to be envisioning his own song from *Of Thee I Sing*, "Posterity Is Just Around the Corner," in this memorable Van Vechten photograph. (Van Vechten Collection, Library of Congress Prints and Photographs Division.)

Oscar Levant Plays in Pittsburgh. Oscar Levant had a substantial acting career, mostly playing versions of himself in musically oriented films, and was a notorious wit on radio and television. As an interpreter of Gershwin's music, his concert and recording career thrived. Levant, born in Pittsburgh, was Gershwin's friend and musical associate, and his understanding of the Gershwin style made him a natural choice for playing Gershwin after the composer's death. His pianism highlighted the 1939 Gershwin memorial concert at the City College of New York's Lewisohn Stadium. Levant, shown here in a scene from *The Barkleys of Broadway*, continued to interpret Gershwin's music for decades after the Lewisohn concerts, often with the Pittsburgh Symphony. On November 24 and 26, 1939, under musical director Fritz Reiner, Levant played the *Concerto in F* and premiered his own composition, *Dirge* ("In Memory of George Gershwin"). Reporting on the concert, Pittsburgh's *Musical Forecast* magazine noted of Levant, "His deep-rooted friendship with the late, lamented George Gershwin, and his innate understanding of the spirit of Gershwin's compositions, so admirably reflected in his public performances of Gershwin's piano works, have identified Oscar with Gershwin in the public consciousness." Among Levant's other Pittsburgh Symphony appearances, usually with Gershwin works, were those in November 1941, April 1947, and January 1950.

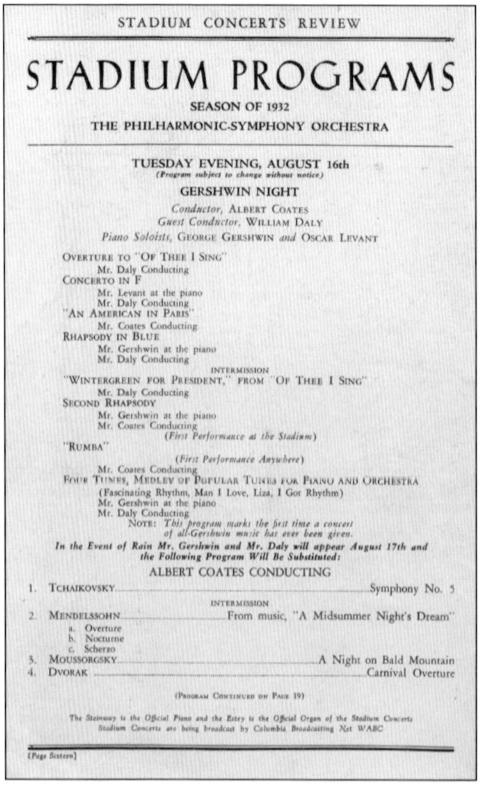

STADIUM CONCERTS REVIEW

STADIUM PROGRAMS

SEASON OF 1932

THE PHILHARMONIC-SYMPHONY ORCHESTRA

TUESDAY EVENING, AUGUST 16th

(Program subject to change without notice)

GERSHWIN NIGHT

Conductor, ALBERT COATES

Guest Conductor, WILLIAM DALY

Piano Soloists, GEORGE GERSHWIN *and* OSCAR LEVANT

OVERTURE TO "OF THEE I SING"
Mr. Daly Conducting

CONCERTO IN F
Mr. Levant at the piano
Mr. Daly Conducting

"AN AMERICAN IN PARIS"
Mr. Coates Conducting

RHAPSODY IN BLUE
Mr. Gershwin at the piano
Mr. Daly Conducting

INTERMISSION

"WINTERGREEN FOR PRESIDENT," FROM "OF THEE I SING"
Mr. Daly Conducting

SECOND RHAPSODY
Mr. Gershwin at the piano
Mr. Coates Conducting
(First Performance at the Stadium)

"RUMBA"
(First Performance Anywhere)
Mr. Coates Conducting

FOUR TUNES, MEDLEY OF POPULAR TUNES FOR PIANO AND ORCHESTRA
(Fascinating Rhythm, Man I Love, Liza, I Got Rhythm)
Mr. Gershwin at the piano
Mr. Daly Conducting

NOTE: *This program marks the first time a concert of all-Gershwin music has ever been given.*

In the Event of Rain Mr. Gershwin and Mr. Daly will appear August 17th and the Following Program Will Be Substituted:

ALBERT COATES CONDUCTING

1. TCHAIKOVSKY .... Symphony No. 5

INTERMISSION

2. MENDELSSOHN .... From music, "A Midsummer Night's Dream"
   a. Overture
   b. Nocturne
   c. Scherzo
3. MOUSSORGSKY .... A Night on Bald Mountain
4. DVORAK .... Carnival Overture

(PROGRAM CONTINUED ON PAGE 19)

The Steinway is the Official Piano and the Estey is the Official Organ of the Stadium Concerts
Stadium Concerts are being broadcast by Columbia Broadcasting Net WABC

[Page Sixteen]

LEWISOHN STADIUM GERSHWIN NIGHT PROGRAM, 1932. The first concert at the City College of New York's stadium for which Oscar Levant joined Gershwin in performing was in August 1932. The program proclaims that the evening "marks the first time a concert of all-Gershwin music has ever been given." There were two conductors: William Daly and Albert Coates. The *Cuban Overture* was given its premiere performance at this concert. Initially, that piece was called *Rumba.*

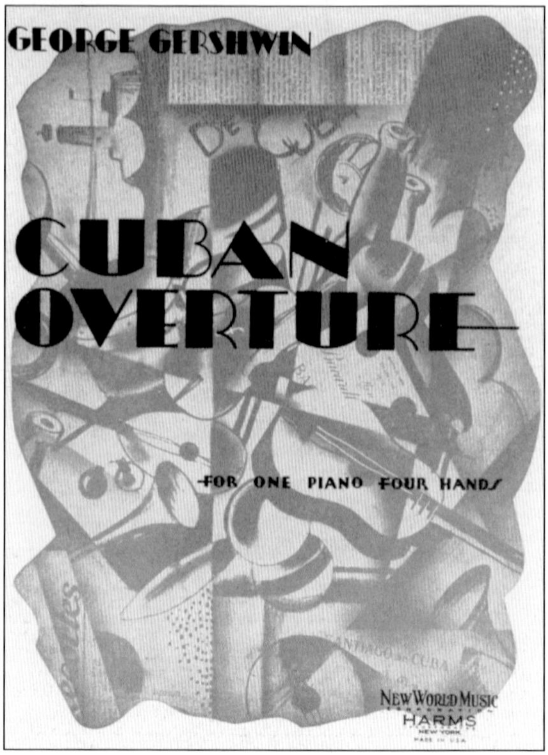

SHEET MUSIC FOR *CUBAN OVERTURE*, 1932. Perhaps inspired by the Cuban-flavored music popularized by bandleader Xavier Cugat that he heard at New York's Waldorf-Astoria, Gershwin, in early 1932, vacationed in Havana with several friends—with the direct purpose of studying Cuban music for a new composition. As with *An American in Paris*, he returned home with souvenirs that would be incorporated into what he first called *Rumba:* a set of authentic Cuban percussion instruments. Within a few months, he changed the title to *Cuban Overture.*

FRITZ REINER (1888–1963). The conductor of the Pittsburgh Symphony Orchestra from 1938 to 1948, Reiner had a long association with Gershwin and his music. He invited Gershwin to perform with his Cincinnati Symphony in 1927 and Oscar Levant to play his and Gershwin's works in 1939 and 1941. Reiner also commissioned Robert Russell Bennett—the orchestrator of several Gershwin stage and movie musicals—to create *Porgy and Bess: A Symphonic Picture*, which the Pittsburgh Symphony premiered in February 1943. (Library of Congress Prints and Photographs Division.)

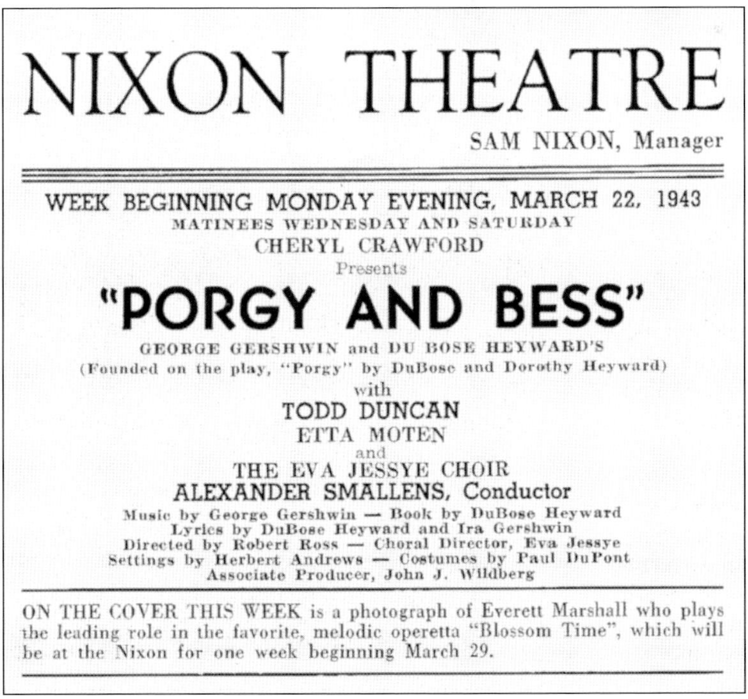

ADVERTISEMENT FOR *PORGY AND BESS* REVIVAL AT THE NIXON THEATRE, 1943. The so-called "Cheryl Crawford revival" of *Porgy and Bess* returned the opera to Broadway in January 1942, shortening and editing the work and replacing the recitative with spoken dialogue. This version attracted increased appreciation and popularity, sending *Porgy and Bess* back to the Nixon Theatre in March 1943.

Rhapsody in Blue Poster and Press Pass, 1945. This elaborate film biography (Warner Bros.) stars Robert Alda as Gershwin and contains a plethora of Gershwin music—with even a version of his mini-opera *Blue Monday*. Many friends and associates of the composer played themselves, including Oscar Levant, George White, and Paul Whiteman. Also shown is a rare pass for the Warner Bros. "press review" screening.

SCENE FROM *RHAPSODY IN BLUE*. *Rhapsody in Blue* marked the first of many Gershwin-related films in which Oscar Levant appeared, often playing himself—here in a *Rhapsody in Blue* scene with Robert Alda—or a version of his wisecracking, piano-playing persona. Alda also acted in *The Man I Love*, a 1947 film-noir classic using Gershwin's famous song thematically.

THE BARKLEYS OF BROADWAY POSTER, 1949. This last Astaire-Rogers movie (MGM) was a 10-year reunion of sorts, as their RKO partnership had ended with 1939's *The Story of Vernon and Irene Castle*. In *Barkleys*, the pair plays a married theatrical couple; Oscar Levant is also featured. Gershwin had complained about the "throwaway" treatment accorded "They Can't Take That Away from Me" in its original *Shall We Dance* setting. Under the gaze of Ira Gershwin (the film's lyricist, to music by Harry Warren), the song was given its deserved prominence.

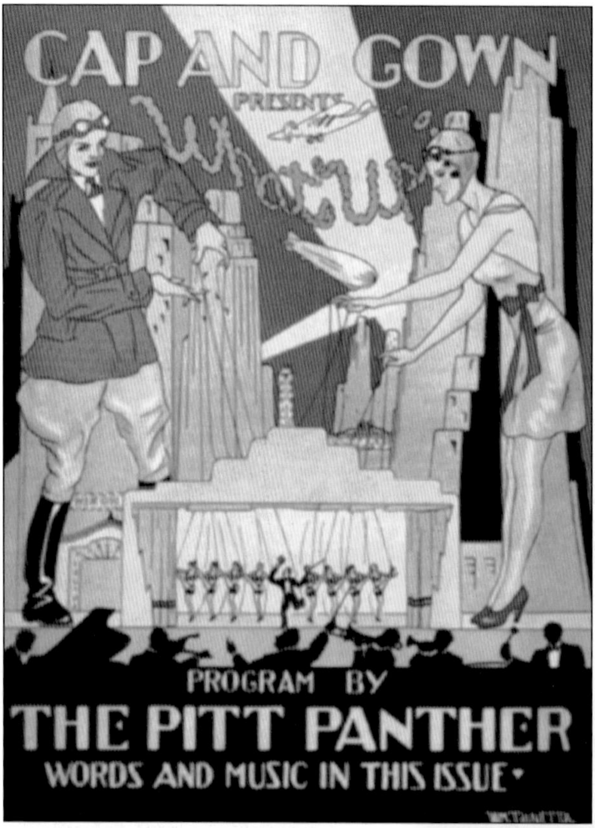

GENE KELLY (1912–1996) AT PITT. Gene Kelly was from the Highland Park and Point Breeze neighborhoods of the Steel City and attended the University of Pittsburgh. While at Pitt, Kelly was involved with the Cap and Gown Club, which produced annual musicals. After he graduated in 1933, Kelly returned to become the productions' director. Each year, the April issue of the *Pitt Panther* magazine served as the program for the Cap and Gown production. The 1931 issue shown highlights *What's Up*, Kelly's first Pitt show as a dancing performer. Dr. Benjamin Levant—Oscar's brother—wrote the music for Kelly's dance routine "Happy Rhythm" in *What's Up*.

GENE KELLY AT THE NIXON THEATRE, 1938. This nighttime view of the Nixon Theatre's marquee announces the Cap and Gown Club's *Pickets, Please!* Gene Kelly directed that April 1938 production, his last at Pitt. Kelly taught at and managed the Gene Kelly Studio of the Dance in the city's Squirrel Hill neighborhood in the mid-1930s. (Pitt Photographs, University of Pittsburgh Historic Photographs, University of Pittsburgh.)

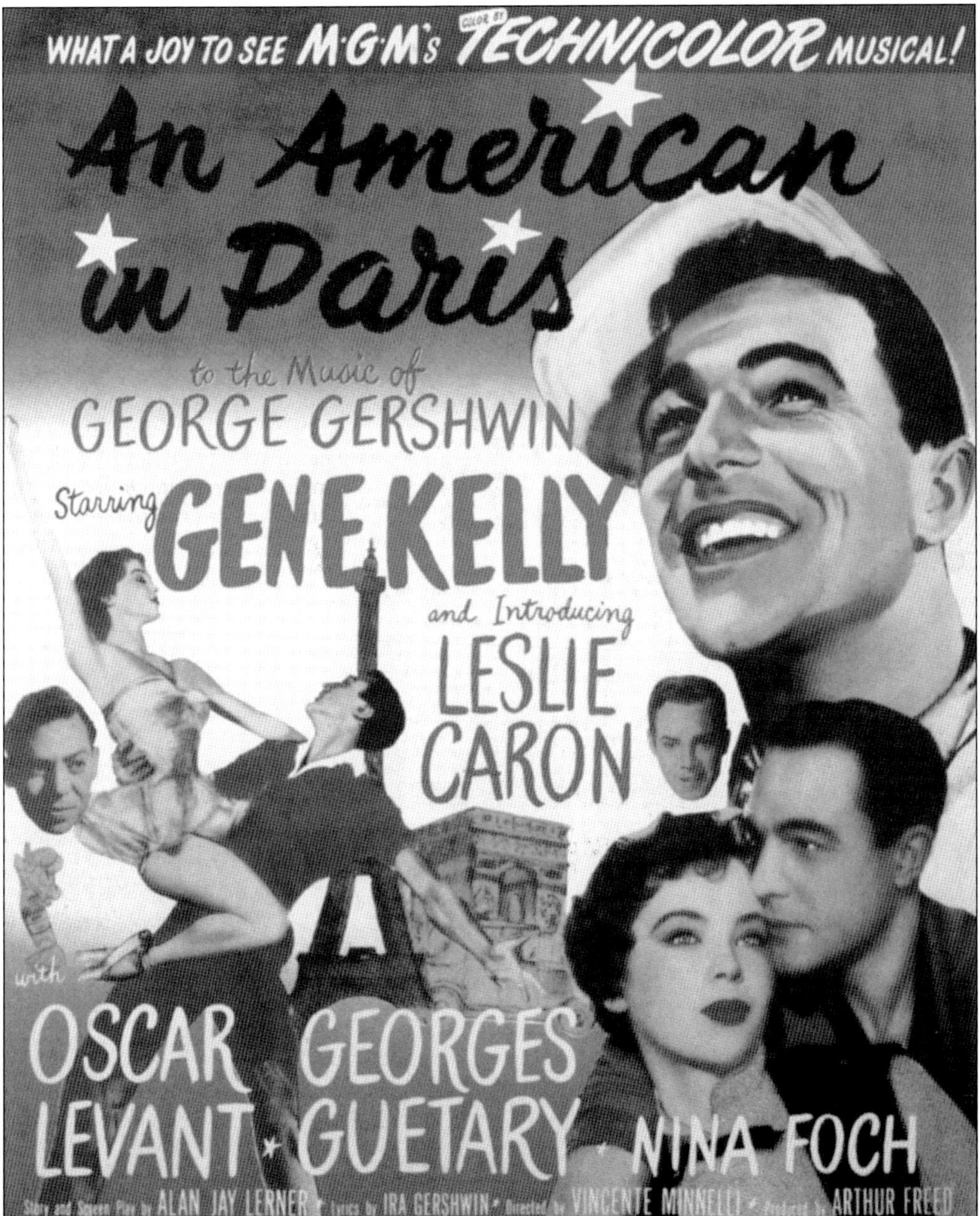

AN AMERICAN IN PARIS WINDOW CARD, 1951. This award-winning movie musical (MGM) represented Gene Kelly's ambitious project for a film based entirely on George Gershwin's music. The centerpiece is a long ballet to *An American in Paris*; Kelly constructed the dances to match scenes and themes derived from the works of great French artists. Oscar Levant joined him in a Pittsburgh-native one-two punch to pay the ultimate cinematic homage to the beloved composer.

Maxine Sullivan (1911–1987). Born Marietta Williams in Homestead, jazz singer Maxine Sullivan cemented her fame with her stirring performance at the 1938 Lewisohn Stadium memorial concert on the first anniversary of George Gershwin's passing. With the Paul Whiteman Orchestra and the New York Philharmonic-Symphony, Maxine thrilled the audience of 20,000 (and radio-broadcast listeners) with her renditions of "Summertime" and four encore songs.

Earl Wild (1915–2010). Pittsburgh-born pianist Earl Wild first performed Gershwin's *Rhapsody in Blue* in 1942 with Arturo Toscanini. With Arthur Fiedler's Boston Pops Orchestra, he produced an RCA Living Stereo LP featuring *Rhapsody in Blue* and *An American in Paris* in 1960 and, in 1962, an RCA LP compiling *Cuban Overture*, *Concerto in F*, and the then-little-known *"I Got Rhythm" Variations*. Wild wrote *Seven Virtuoso Etudes* after Gershwin songs, a *Theme and Variations on George Gershwin's "Someone to Watch Over Me,"* and *Grand Fantasy on Porgy and Bess*.

Lorin Maazel (1930–2014). The world-famous conductor Lorin Maazel was from Pittsburgh, and though his relation to Gershwin's music is relatively modest, the groundbreaking recording he supervised with the Cleveland Orchestra and Chorus of *Porgy and Bess* is of paramount importance. Of the many recorded versions of the opera, this was the first in which Gershwin's original vision was honored, with all the scenes and music included. Billed as the "World Premiere Complete Recording," it unveiled extraordinary passages never before revealed other than in Gershwin's written score.

André Previn (1929–2019). Music director and conductor of the Pittsburgh Symphony Orchestra from 1976 to 1984, André Previn was related to Charles Previn, who had conducted many of Gershwin's concerts and musicals. André hosted the series *Previn and the Pittsburgh* in 1977 on PBS television. He made several recordings of Gershwin works with the Pittsburgh Symphony, was the conductor for the 1959 *Porgy and Bess* movie, and was guest pianist for the New York Philharmonic's 1998 concert "Gershwin at the Philharmonic: Celebrating the 100th Birthday of George Gershwin."

THREE GERSHWIN THEATER/CONCERT PROGRAMS, 2010S. In recent years, Pittsburgh has continued its love affair with Gershwin. A few of these music events are revealed through the programs shown. " 'S Wonderful," a revue-type celebration of Gershwin songs, was presented by the Pittsburgh Civic Light Opera in June 2010. Pittsburgh Ballet Theatre's "A Gershwin Fantasy: Shall We Dance" (March 2011) was a new ballet sponsored by Pittsburgh educator and arts philanthropist Richard E. Rauh, who has provided endowments for numerous Jewish and cultural organizations; he is the grandson of Bertha Rauh, one of the city's leading citizens earlier in the 20th century, who had welcomed George Gershwin into her home after his 1933 Syria Mosque concert. The Pittsburgh Pops' "Here to Stay: The Gershwin Experience" (June 2012) was supervised and conducted by Marvin Hamlisch (1944–2012). This author was involved with both of the latter productions, having been asked to prepare accompanying exhibitions at the Heinz Hall and Byham Theater venues. The "Here to Stay" concert marked a renewal of an association with Marvin Hamlisch, who wrote the foreword to the author's 1998 book *Gershwin in His Time*.

GEORGE GERSHWIN, 1937. This last photograph of Gershwin performing was taken at RKO at the end of June 1937. "Old music and new music, forgotten melodies and the craze of the moment, bits of opera, Russian folk songs, Spanish ballads, chansons, rag-time ditties combined in a mighty chorus in my inner ear," Gershwin once wrote. "And through and over it all I heard, faint at first, loud at last, the soul of this great America of ours." (Museum of Modern Art Film Stills Archive.)

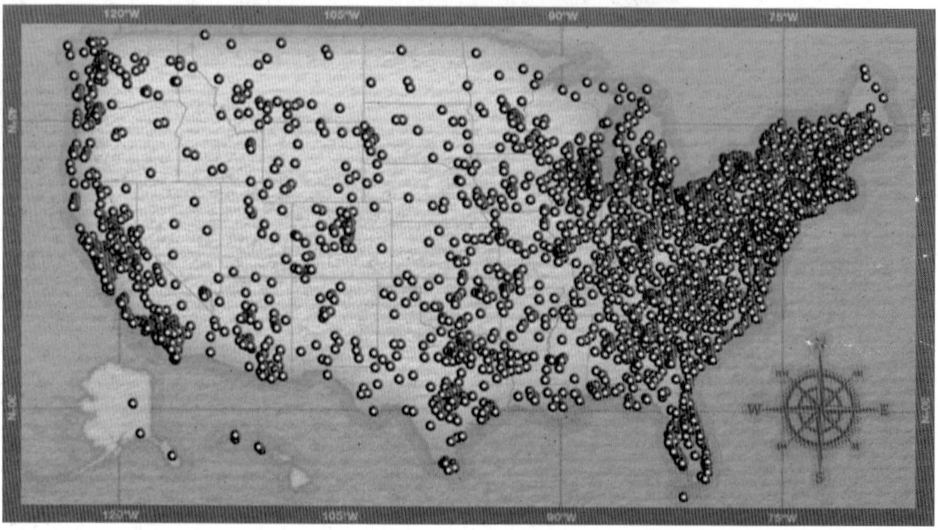